AF521941

PREACHING FROM GENESIS

PREACHING FROM GENESIS

The Perfecting of the Believer's Faith

J.W. LEE

BAKER BOOK HOUSE
Grand Rapids, Michigan

ISBN: 0-8010-5542-3

PHOTOLITHOPRINTED BY CUSHING - MALLOY, INC.
ANN ARBOR, MICHIGAN, UNITED STATES OF AMERICA
1975

Contents

Preface

Due to the encouragement of students whom I led in an intensive study of Genesis, I agreed to prepare a series of sermon outlines on this great book. The task has proven to be a difficult but an enjoyable one.

The work represented by the following outlines has been done in varied surroundings. They represent the work of a student as I studied under Dr. J. Wash Watts in New Orleans Baptist Theological Seminary. Some of the outlines are expansions of the wonderful theological truths that he concluded from his study of the Scriptures.[1] Most of the outlines represent the work of a pastor who must constantly study under the pressure of multiplying demands. These represent an effort to educate a church in the truths of this book and also to encourage them to live out these truths in their daily lives. Yet other outlines reflect the work of a teacher who seeks to lead his students to take ancient truths and make them relevant to modern-day living.

In each case the work has been done under the pressure of many other responsibilities. It does not reflect the work of one who withdrew in seclusion from other tasks in order to complete the work. The demands of a busy schedule would not permit this.

The primary purpose of making these outlines available is to lend assistance to the busy pastor who wishes to share the great treasures of this first book of our Bible with his congregation. By no means is this intended to be an exhaustive sermonic treatment of the entire book. Instead, it is one approach out of many in developing the major themes and theological truths of Genesis. Some of these outlines are expositional outlines of chapters, while others are presented topically with the material in a given chapter or event serving as background. Some of the outlines may also prove helpful on certain occasions such as on Father's Day or in a stewardship emphasis. Basically the author desires that this work may be used to exalt Christ in the life of each person who studies it.

Another purpose is to lend assistance to the student as he studies Genesis. By referring to these outlines as he studies the Biblical text, he may grasp an insight into the emphasis of a given chapter or section of Genesis.

A suggested plan for using these outlines is for the student to read in at

[1]Note the sermons on pages 5, 9, and 13 and pages 10, 11, 26, and 27 in J. Wash Watts, *Old Testament Teaching,* 1967, and pages 38-46 and 50-58 in Watts, *Glimpses of God,* 1957.

least two translations the Biblical material that is covered. A copy of J. Wash Watts, *Old Testament Teaching* (Broadman Press, 1967), though limited in his comments on various passages, will prove helpful in areas with which he dealt. Two or more commentaries should also be used. Some of these that will prove helpful are as follows: Derek Kidner, *Genesis, An Introduction and Commentary* (Inter-Varsity Press, 1972); Gerhard von Rad, *Genesis* (The Westminster Press, 1961); W. H. Griffith Thomas, *Genesis, A Devotional Commentary* (Wm. B. Eerdmans Publishing Company, 1969); Charles F. Pfeiffer, *The Book of Genesis* (Baker Book House, 1970); and H. C. Leupold, *Exposition of Genesis* (Baker Book House, 1970). The reading of this material will give one additional insights and background to the outlines.

I am grateful for the encouragement and assistance granted by persons too numerous to list. My desire is that at the completion of studying these outlines the reader may feel that his time has been well spent and that he can better "divide the word of truth."

Through the entire book of Genesis one can note the spiritual progress in the lives of individuals. With frankness and candidness the records bear testimony of sin in the lives of these believers, but they also reveal that God worked with them to perfect their faith. As their faith was perfected, their lives also reflected it. This truth is illustrated in the lives of Adam and Eve, Noah, Abraham, Isaac, Jacob, Joseph, and Judah. That which was true in their lives is the promise to the Christian as recorded in Philippians 1:6: "Being confident of this very thing, that he which hath begun a good work in you will perform [perfect] it until the day of Jesus Christ."

My desire is that the Spirit of God may breathe upon these outlines, upon you, and upon those with whom you may share them to perfect the faith of each person that his life may reflect Christ who has come to reveal God to man.

3

The Author of Salvation

Genesis 3:1-19

Within this passage we find the *protevangelium,* or the first gospel. God gave it after sin had marred the "image of God" in His creatures. Unlike the parent who refuses to aid a child whom he feels has disgraced his name, God goes looking for Adam and Eve. He does not wait for man to seek Him. He seeks man. Listen to His voice as He calls, "Adam, Adam, where are you?" He knows, but He wants Adam to realize where he is. Man must recognize his lost, sinful condition.

Three parties are involved in this human tragedy that occurs daily. Let's consider how God deals with each of them.

I. *The Serpent: ultimate damnation is pronounced upon him.*
  A. His offense (3:1-6).
    1. He engaged in subtlety.
      a. His first question was suggestive, insinuating that God is less than love.
      b. The word "subtle" means to be artful, and describes a well-laid plan that kills: such as by stripping bark from a tree or skin from a living person.
    2. He expressed falsehoods and lies (3:1, 4).
      a. He sought to raise doubt.
        (1) Doubt concerning the love of God for His creatures.
        (2) Doubt concerning the authority of God's word.
        (3) Doubt concerning the certainty of judgment.
      b. He sought to elicit desire (3:6a).
        (1) Self-satisfaction became Eve's goal.
        (2) Fulfillment of personal desire is the major goal of the "new morality."
      c. He sought to encourage disobedience (3:6b).
        (1) Eve hoped to become as God, but failed.
        (2) Then she knew sin, not as God knows it, but by experience.
        (3) Today men still pursue this goal of self-deification. Humanism is on the upswing.
    3. He exhibited maliciousness.
      a. There was no guilt, shame, pity, or sorrow.
      b. He is the same today. He leaves a trail of broken promises.
  B. The curse (3:14-15). (The inherent character of the serpent is described.)

1. His nature: degraded (3:14).
   a. His mode of conveyance: "upon thy belly."
   b. His method of existence: "dust shalt thou eat."
2. His defeat: certain (3:15). (God's supernatural work would effect it.)
   a. God initiated the warfare.
   b. God will accomplish the victory.
   c. God encourages the struggle. ("Enmity" is personal antagonism aroused by God.)
   d. God described it as a spiritual warfare.
   e. God predicted the victory in this personal warfare through a Promised Seed—Christ (Galatians 3:16).
      (1) The type of warfare is a struggle to the death.
      (2) The outcome of the warfare is a crushed head (defeat) for Satan.

II. *The woman: the author of salvation is provided through her* (3:16). (She had become a temptress to Adam.)
   A. The consequence of sin would be suffered by her.
      1. Increased pain in her most sublime achievement—childbirth.
      2. Desire for her husband.
      3. Subjection under her husband's authority. (Where sin is rampant the subjection of woman is most evident.)
   B. The Conqueror of sin, the Saviour, would come through her.

III. *The man: the possibility of salvation is provided for him* (3:17-19). (Adam, the spiritual leader, fell into sin because of Eve, 3:17a.)
   A. The ground was cursed (3:18).
      1. To discipline man.
      2. To develop man's spirituality by leading him to sense his need for God.
   B. The penalty for sin was specified.
      1. To experience endless, unproductive toil. (The word for "toil" is the same word as "pain." It may also be translated "travail.")
      2. To expect the prospect of death. (To return to the dust is an indication of mortality.)
   C. The prospect of salvation was promised.
      1. To lift man from the depths of despair.
      2. To encourage man to anticipate deliverance through the Promised Seed of the woman.

IV. *The God: the provision of hope and salvation is by Him.*
   A. He was offended by man's rebellion.
   B. He was concerned for man's needs. He diligently seeks sinners.
   C. He disciplined man for sin. His discipline was designed to secure repentance.
   D. He promised victory in the ultimate battle so as to inspire assurance in the warfare with Satan.

4

The Promise of the Messiah

Genesis 3:14-15

In the book *Through the Valley of the Kwai,* Ernest Gordon compared Christmas of 1942 with Christmas of 1943. In 1942 at Christmas the men were stealing food from the sick and eating it themselves. In 1943 the men met on Christmas for worship, sang carols, prayed, and read Scripture. What made the difference? Dr. Gordon called it "the miracle of the Kwai." *One* man had begun caring for a sick friend. He took his own meager rations and gave them to his sick friend. The man who was well grew ill and died. The sick man recovered. Men began to think of Christ who said, "Greater love hath no man than this. . . ." As a result many were converted in that prisoner of war camp.

Down through the ages men have longed and looked for a person or means by which they could be reconciled to God and to one another. They have earnestly desired someone to bear away their guilt and to bring peace to their hearts. This was a Jewish expectation from early times; it was the pagan's hallucination which he could not quite comprehend; and now it is the Christian's realization.

The giving of Messiah was not according to a haphazard plan, but it was a divine plan. That plan was first given in the garden of Eden in the initial announcement of the good news which has been fulfilled in the person of Jesus Christ.

The promise of the Saviour:

I. *Reveals the condition of man.*
  A. Dead, as a result of sin. Man is out of fellowship with God.
    1. Evident in his disobedience. He declares, "I'll do as I please."
    2. Evident in his dishonesty. He deceives himself by passing sin off as fun rather than as folly.
    3. Evident in his departure from God. He is hiding from Him hoping to cover up the nakedness of sin with a fig leaf! But God does not look on the outward appearance.
    4. Evident in his deification of self. He attempts to dethrone God.
  B. Divisive, as a consequence of sin. Man is at enmity with his fellowman.
    1. Adam turned against Eve. The home was disrupted.
    2. Cain rose up against Abel. Normal family relationships were destroyed.
  C. Desperate, as a penalty for sin. Man was driven from the garden.
    1. Fallen man needed to be restored to a right relationship with God.
    2. Estranged man needed to be made at peace with one another.

3. The angelic choir sang of this in the announcement of the Saviour's birth. Peace will be found as men find it in Christ.

II. *Reflects the character of God* (15:6).

A. The faithfulness of God is revealed. God will be true to His Word and Himself.

1. He is not capricious, but consistent.
2. He is never changing, but changeless.

B. The holiness of God is manifested.

1. He cannot regard sin with impunity.
2. He reveals sin to be a barrier separating God from man.

C. The lovingkindness of God is disclosed. He mercifully acts in grace to withhold punishment.

1. He is aware of man's need for spiritual help.
2. He acts in promising and producing the Messiah, our Saviour.
   a. He was predicted to be of woman's seed (3:15). Eve would lead out in this struggle.
   b. He was described as the Rightful Ruler (49:10). Judah's line was to be the lineage of His descent.

III. *Results in the reconciliation of man to God* (4:26).

A. Divine discipline of the disobedient children was provided (3:24).

B. A divine diagnosis of sin's effect on Woman and on Man was made (3:16-19).

1. To lead man to a dependence upon God. "For your sake" God did this.
2. To win man to a renewed faith in Him.

C. Divine destruction of Satan and his seed, i.e., his followers, was promised.

1. No hope whatsoever was provided for him, but he was to be defeated by the Messiah.
2. This was accomplished on the cross by Christ who declared, "It is perfected."

Thus the condition of man and the character of God prompted the sending of the Messiah. Men of old looked forward and longed for the coming of the Messiah. These all "died in faith." Today we look back to the coming of the Messiah in Christ Jesus. For us it must be in faith—faith in Him as the answer to the ills of our world and the sin of our lives.

5

The God of Providential Care

Genesis 3:20–4:26 (Matthew 6:31-33)

By listening to and heeding the serpent, man fell from his original state of innocence and security. Looking over the serpent's head, so to speak, God had pronounced Satan's defeat and cursed him in man's presence. This was to inspire hope in man. Then God did not leave man to his fate, but continued to work with man to encourage his return to God in repentance, faith, and love. By His acts He revealed Himself as the God who cares.

There was:

I. *Providential helpfulness: provision of clothing* (3:21).
  A. The slaying of an animal was not sacrificial. Such laws came much later.
  B. Primarily this was a meaningful act of kindness and mercy.
    1. Self-made clothing covered their nakedness with flimsy fig leaves.
    2. God-given clothing provided protection which was sufficient.
    3. Divine love was expressed in a practical way. (But nature was disrupted by the death of some animal to meet man's need.)

II. *Providential discipline: expulsion from the garden* (3:22-24).
  A. God first dealt with man's physical needs; then with man's spiritual condition.
  B. Sin brought the punishment of expulsion from Paradise, i.e., separation from God's presence.
    1. To prevent unending continuance in sin (3:22).
    2. To be executed by a loving God, not by blind fate (3:23a).
    3. To be experienced universally (3:24). "All have sinned."
    4. To redeem rebellious man from sin.

III. *Providential favor: acceptance of an offering brought in faith* (4:1-4).
  A. The purpose of offerings was to effect reconciliation.
  B. Abel sought to escape sin's power while Cain sought to escape sin's penalty.
  C. Abel was reconciled to God because in faith he put God first (4:4; Hebrews 11:4).

IV. *Providential rebuke: rejection of an offering not brought in faith* (4:5-7).
  A. God's refusal to accept the offering was because of Cain's lack of faith (4:7).
    1. Even prescribed offerings are bribes if brought by unbelievers.

2. Offerings must be brought in faith and love to be a blessing to the giver.

B. God's warning was intended to inspire faith (4:7).

V. *Providential mercy: appointment of a sign for Cain* (4:8-15).

A. The curse on the ground was intended to discipline Cain (4:9-12).

B. Cain's rebellion against such discipline indicated an inherent instability (4:12a).

C. Cain thought that he could not be forgiven, and that he would be killed (4:13).

D. God rejected Cain's conclusions by saying, "Not so!" (4:15). (The "mark" was God's pledge of protection.)

VI. *Providential prediction: results of Cain's sin* (4:16-24).

A. The influence of sin grows oppressive upon those refusing to deal with it.

B. The progress of sin reached a peak in Cain's grandson, Lamech (4:23-24).

1. Separation from God.
2. Disruption of the marital state.
3. Hypocrisy in worship.
4. Manslaughter.
5. Instability of character.
6. A life without roots, ever wandering.
7. Polygamy.
8. Murder.

VII. *Providential effect: beginning of the worship of Yahweh* (4:25-26).

A. The causes of worship.

1. The prevalence of sin and violence.
2. The providential care of God.

B. The basis for worship.

1. God's revelation of Himself as the Faithful One. (The name *Seth* means "Appointed One." It reflected man's hope in the Promised Seed.)
2. Man's recognition of Yahweh God as the Sustainer of Life. (The name *Enos* means "Mortal One.")

6
The Effects of Sin

Genesis 4:7-8, 16-24

Shortly after the creation Satan began striving for the destruction of man. Sin soon entered the world through the disobedience of Eve. Then everything Satan promised vanished as though it were smoke. Man did not become as God, knowing good and evil, but a person estranged from God, yet dependent upon God's mercy.

Furthermore, sin—that soul-killing spiritual cancer that Satan would have us believe is harmless—continued its devastating work in the offspring of our first parents. In Cain and his descendants we see the full effect of sin revealing itself. Three effects brought about by sin are seen in this account.

Sin is:

I. *Universal in its extent.*
   A. Even in Abel's life sin's influence was expressed.
      1. He felt the need for reconciliation to God.
      2. He felt compelled to express his desire through a sacrifice.
      3. He was delivered from sin's penalty by faith (Hebrews 11:4).
   B. Even in the lives of God's chosen people sin was evident.
      1. It was present in differing degrees (e.g., of those listed in chapters 4 and 5 *only* Enoch was translated).
      2. It was in Noah's life.
         a. Before the flood (6:8-9).
         b. After the flood (9:20 f.).
   C. Even in our lives today sin is a reality (Romans 3:23).
      1. Sin is no respecter of persons.
      2. We all face it daily.

II. *Damning in its effect* (Romans 6:23). Even when it is checked it produces sorrow.
   A. In the lives of men.
      1. Sin produced sorrow for Adam as he toiled daily and as he viewed Abel's dead body.
      2. Sin, unchecked, led Cain to become a murderer, fugitive, wanderer, and vagabond.
         a. Cain's life was ruined.
         b. Men's lives are still restless and ruined when sin runs unchecked.
      3. Sin affected the lives of Cain's children (4:16-24).
         a. Lamech.
            (1) Sin's degrading effect on family life led to polygamy.
            (2) Sin's dehumanizing effect on social life led to murder.

(a) Life was considered cheap.
(b) Life became miserable.

b. Descendants of Cain (6:5). (Sin's effect is seen in full bloom when man's daily existence became a living hell.)
   (1) Immorality and wickedness abounded as a result of marriage between true worshipers and Cain's descendants.
   (2) Immorality and ungodliness always abound as elements of hell where sin reigns. (After walking down Bourbon Street in New Orleans, Billy Graham said, "I thought that I was in hell.")

B. To the souls of men.
   1. To the serpent, Satan (3:14 f.). "You are going to hell," i.e., a place of final destruction.
   2. To his seed. Those who follow Satan are to suffer eternal damnation (Revelation 20:12-15).

III. *Overcome only by faith in the Lord.*

A. Adam and Eve met and overcame sin by faith in Yahweh God. They exercised *simple trust.*
   1. Eve expressed her faith in the words "with the help of Yahweh."
   2. Eve entered the valley of the shadow of death in childbirth and realized that the Lord was with her to bring her through it.
   3. Eve recognized the handiwork of God in her new-born baby (4:1).

B. Seth overcame sin by faith in the Lord. He exercised *simple trust.*
   1. The meaning of *Yahweh* to Seth was "The Preserver of Life" (4:26).
   2. The experience of worship enabled Seth to overcome sin's power and penalty.

C. Noah overcame sin in the same way. He exercised *simple trust.*
   1. Noah offered sacrifices on the day that he left the ark (8:20).
   2. His sacrifices pointed to the blood of Christ "which taketh away the sins of the world."

D. Man overcomes sin today in the same way. He must exercise *simple trust.*

7

The God Who Inspires Worship

Genesis 5:1– 6:8

God had urged man to take of the Tree of Life and live, but man had rebelled. As a result of his sin, man began to sense a new need for God. Through chastening and providential leading God inspired man to return to Him through worship.

The literary heading of Genesis 5:1–6:8 indicates the unity of this section. Its unity is not biological, for Cain and his descendants are not named. Neither are the first-born sons listed. The unity is that of a Community of Faith. These men, popularly noted for their longevity, were primarily leaders in the worship of God.

In their experiences we see:

I. *The reasons for worship.*
   A. The fact of creation (Psalm 19:1).
      1. The beauty of a sunrise arouses man's thoughts of God.
      2. The grandeur of the Rocky Mountains leads one to proclaim "How Great Thou Art!" (a hymn by Stuart K. Hine).
   B. The fact of God's providence (Psalm 103; 148:1-5).
   C. The fact of sin.
      1. Man's sin is basically a rejection of God, and an indication of pride as man deifies self.
      2. Man's sin results in a lack of direction. (Augustine declared: "Our hearts are restless, and we cannot find rest until we find rest in thee.")
   D. The fact of danger and uncertainty.
      1. Mortal danger was posed by rebellious sinners. "Is this vile world a friend to grace, To help me on to God?" (I. Watts).
      2. Men desired providential protection of their lives.
   E. The yearning for divine fellowship.

II. *The principles of worship.* (The names of ten men who were leaders in worship span the time from Adam to Noah.)
   A. Worship in the Lord's name (Yahweh) was begun by *Seth* and *Enos* (4:26).
   B. Worship includes several factors which are indicated by the names or actions of these men.
      1. Praise.
         a. *Kenan* means "A Flute Player," or "Hymn Singer."
         b. *Mahalalel* means "Praise."
      2. Prayer. *Jared* means "One Who Prostrated," or "Bowed Down."
      3. Preaching.

a. *Methuselah* possibly means "A Man Sent," or "A Messenger."

b. Ministry of *Noah* included preaching.

4. Consecration. *Enoch* means "Dedicated," or "Trained One."
5. Giving. This is evident in the offering of *Abel* in Genesis 4:4.

III. *The results of worship.*

A. Fellowship with God.

1. Symbolized by Enoch's walking with God.
2. Exemplified in Noah's personal communion with God.

B. Communication from God.

1. Enoch learned how to walk close to God in an evil age.
2. God's will was clearly revealed to Noah.

C. Comfort and joy in God. (In the face of danger and death these were known.)

D. Separation from the world.

1. From worldly corruption (e.g., Enoch, who lived in the age of Lamech, was but one generation from the flood, yet he was translated).
2. From worldly religion (4:22, 24; 6:2). (This is indicated by the worship of *Ha'Elohim,* The One True God.)

E. Victory in life. Longevity of life was experienced by these men.

F. Victory over death.

Billy Graham in *World Aflame* said, "Either man began nowhere and is looking for some place to go, or he began somewhere with some place to go but has lost the way." God leads men to find the way, and as they do, their hearts are lifted up in true worship of Him.

8
The God of Judgment
Genesis 6:1-8

Speculation and misunderstanding have characterized much of the proposed interpretations of Genesis 6. Although the marriage of angelic beings is never indicated in other passages of Scripture, and in spite of Christ's word that in heaven there is neither marriage nor giving in marriage, some expositors contend that Genesis 6 tells of heavenly creatures who in unbridled lust took human wives and begot superhuman children who became giants. Such interpretation, if accurate, would reflect the ingredients of idolatry, immorality, and polytheism. The author of Genesis, however, is concerned with monotheism. For those who accept this as inspired Scripture and feel that no mythology is contained in this record, such interpretation is unacceptable. Another one is possible and is in accord with the revealed facts.

To our own detriment we have failed to place the judgment of God in its proper perspective. We have magnified His graciousness, love, mercy, patience, and understanding; but what about His judgment? Christ spoke of it often and warned men to flee from it.

Since the Bible speaks of judgment, to be true to its message we must acknowledge and prepare for it. God is a holy God, and His holiness must not be ignored. Because He is holy, He is a God of judgment.

The Hebrew word translated "holy" is considered to have originally two possible meanings. One meaning is "bright," designating an object that has been rubbed until all impurities are removed and it shines. The second possible meaning is "separated to," designating that which belongs to God. His absolute holiness demands that He be a God of judgment upon those who are impure or refuse to be separated to Him.

Judgment is a time of separation. It does not come only at some future date, but judgment is in force even now and continues through the future. In Noah's day judgment necessitated separation on the part of believers. The God of Judgment commands and demands separation in all areas of life.

We recognize that He:

I. *Purposes separation in fellowship.*
   A. Rebellious sinners are separated from fellowship with Yahweh.
      1. The evidence of Genesis 2–4 is that those who rebelled were driven away.
      2. The teaching of Genesis 5:1–6:8 is that those who refused to reflect the likeness of God failed to experience fellowship with Him.

3. All those who were ungodly excluded themselves by violence and by corruption.

B. Responsive believers are associated in fellowship with Yahweh.

1. Enoch walked with the One True God *(Ha'Elohim)* (5:22, 24).
2. Noah walked with the One True God (6:8-9).
3. The sons of the One True God were spiritually related in worship to Enoch and Noah, i.e., they walked with God.
   a. They are called "men of the Name" (6:4). This name refers to Yahweh, the Lord, not to "men of renown."
   b. They are designated Mortal Ones, *Enoshim,* and not Mankind, *Ha'adam*.
   c. Thus they were related to Enosh who was among the first to call on the name of the Lord in worship.
4. The daughters of men were those persons who were unresponsive to the leading of God's Spirit (6:3).
5. Separation in fellowship between the godly and the ungodly was a natural result.
   a. Enoch's life was separated from other men.
   b. Noah's life was separated from the other men of his day.

II. *Proposes separation in marriage* (5:32–6:4).

A. Marriage was commonly contracted in Noah's day on the basis of personal appearance and pleasure.

1. Men failed to be concerned over the wicked environment from which their wives came.
2. These women brought evil influences into their new homes.
3. Their unresponsiveness to God revealed their total depravity.
4. A time limit of 120 years was mercifully provided for possible repentance before destruction would come.

B. The *Nephilim* (giants) were separated from such marriages. (The term *Nephilim* may be translated: giants, distinguished ones, invaders, tyrants, fallen ones, or heroes.)

1. They were not the offspring of these marriages (6:4). The perfect verb indicates that they *were,* not *became, Nephilim.*
2. They were Noah and his sons (6:4). "Also after that."
   a. They lived both before and after the flood.
   b. The *Nephilim* were spiritually mighty ones (cf. Psalm 112:1-2). They were "men of the Name" (6:4). Not *renown.*
   c. The *Nephilim* were *separated ones.* (The word *Nephilim* is possibly from the verb "to fall." In Genesis 25:18 it means "to fall away from.")

C. The Christian in our day is directed to refrain from being "unequally yoked" (II Corinthians 6:14).

III. *Promises separation in judgment.*

A. The presence and pervasiveness of evil caused God to repent, i.e., He gave a great sigh.

D. The sign of the Noahic Covenant: the rainbow.

IV. *God orders man's spiritual life* (9:18-27).

A. By exposing the sin of Noah.

1. The Bible presents sin in its ugliness. Noah was drunk and naked.
2. Noah had no previous experience with the vineyard and its potential. (A conclusion reached by Robert Hughes in an unpublished doctoral dissertation at New Orleans Baptist Theological Seminary).
3. Noah personally came to repentance.

B. By condemning the sin of Ham.

1. His sin was not an act of homosexuality, as some have adduced.
2. He expressed a flippant attitude toward sin. (Probably with laughter he told of Noah's condition.)
3. His attitude toward sin had a degrading effect on Canaan.
4. The curse was placed upon Canaan.
   a. It was not a change in skin color.
   b. It was the consequence of sin which was servitude and bondage.

C. By commending the attitude of Shem and Japheth toward sin.

1. They felt a deep sense of shame over their father's plight.
2. They manifested a ready desire to assist in overcoming sin's consequences.
3. Their attitude toward sin would have a beneficent influence on others.
4. The blessing of Noah was given them.
   a. Shem would experience the happiness and peace of Yahweh worship.
   b. Japheth would experience enlargement and liberty by sharing in Yahweh worship.

11

The God Who Guides History

Genesis 10:1–11:9

In the fourth literary division of Genesis, the sacred historian presents "the generations of the sons of Noah." Since the names of chapter 10 are strange to our ears and foreign to our tongues we usually skip the entire section. Nevertheless, it holds pertinent truths for us today. We see:

I. *God warning of the peril of Babylon* (10:1-32).
  A. Descendants of Japheth in the Table of Nations (10:2-5).
    1. The Indo-Germanic races that settled in Europe from Asia Minor and Russia to Wales are Japheth's descendants.
    2. They have contributed to the world the gift of political science, i.e., the extension of government.
  B. Descendants of Ham in the Table of Nations (10:6-20).
    1. The Hamitic races settled primarily from Phoenicia (Lebanon) through Africa.
    2. Some of man's early traces of civilization have come through Egypt.
    3. They have contributed to the world the gift of commerce, i.e., the extension of trade.
  C. Descendants of Shem in the Table of Nations (10:21-31).
    1. The Semitic races settled from Assyria throughout Mesopotamia to Asia Minor and Arabia.
    2. They have contributed to the world the gift of true, revealed monotheism, i.e., the extension of true religion.
      a. Emphasis was placed upon Eber (Crossing Over) as a true follower (10:21).
      b. Emphasis was placed upon Peleg (Division) as an unswerving, stalwart man of faith (10:25).
  D. Nimrod's inclusion in the Table of Nations (10:8-10).
    1. He was known for his personal prowess as a hunter of men. (Such men as Alexander the Great, Constantine, Napoleon, Kaiser Wilhelm, Hitler, Lenin, and Stalin, have reflected such oppressive dictatorship as seen in Nimrod.)
    2. He was known for his political power as the father of Babylon.
      a. Babylon is referred to at least 286 times in Scripture.
      b. It became one of the seven wonders of the world.
      c. Its architectural beauty and hanging gardens were legendary.
      d. It served both as the cradle of ancient civilization and the mortuary of Alexander the Great.

3. His kingdom, Babylon, became synonymous with sin (Revelation 18:21).
4. Cities such as Babylon have customarily been detrimental to God's redemptive purposes.
   a. Sin is multiplied and intensified in cities.
   b. God has usually called His spokesmen from a rural or a small town environment (e.g., Amos, Micah).

II. *God withstanding the presumption of Babel* (11:1-9).
   A. The unity of humanity (11:1-2).
      1. There was a common language.
      2. There was a singleness of purpose.
   B. The dedication of Yahweh's followers.
      1. These persons doubtless offered stiff opposition to the growing unfaithfulness.
      2. Someone such as Shem, Eber, or their followers recorded these events.
   C. The self-exaltation of rebellious sinners.
      1. They determined to build a city, i.e., a city-state or kingdom based on ungodly military oppression.
      2. They determined to build a tower, i.e., a *ziggurat*.
         a. It was a symbol of idolatry as its deity was worshiped.
         b. It was a symbol of immorality as sacred prostitution was incorporated in its ceremonies of worship.
      3. They determined to make a name, i.e., the deification of man.
         a. They desired a worldwide unity to the glorification of man exclusive of God.
         b. They substituted humanism, stark and real, for God.
            (1) Often humanism arises under the disguise of a religion that would *work* its way to heaven.
            (2) Salvation comes first and only by grace, and then results in works.
         c. The deification of man is reflected today in the philosophy of some advocates of world unity and church union.
            (1) We rightfully strive through the United Nations for peace, but that tower beside the East River is as futile as the Tower of Babel to obtain it.
            (2) We recognize that the United Nations' efforts are based on humanism. (The U.N. condemned itself to failure when at its birth at Dumbarton Oaks it refused to acknowledge God in prayer.)
            (3) Our own nation was forged in prayer. But our recognition of God must go deeper and result in righteousness within the fabric of society.
   D. The intervention of God.
      1. He confused their purposes.
      2. He confounded their speech.

3. He condemned their plans (11:8). (They were scattered.)

III. *God working through the promise of Bethlehem.*

A. Through Shem, Eber, Abram, and David, God gave the Promised Messiah (Micah 5:2).

B. Through Christ God meets all our needs for eternity.

C. In Him we see God's ultimate purpose in history (Galatians 4:4 f.).

1. For nations. History is seen as His story.

2. For individuals.

12

The God Who Inspires

Genesis 11:27–12:9

The influence of God's faithful servants had continued for successive generations: Noah, Shem, Japheth, Eber, and Peleg. But this line is always only one generation from extinction.

Associated with this line was Terah, Abram's father. But Terah was not God's servant. He was enamored with the wickedness of Ur, the desire for material gain, and the immoral worship of the moon god.

Into this environment was Abram born. As an obedient son he honored his father, but in his soul was a restiveness, a divine troubling. The witness of Shem and Eber, while incurring no response from Terah, had a deep influence upon Abram. He became sick of the sin of Ur, aware of the inadequacy of material wealth, and convinced of the impotency of idolatry.

God was stirring Abram's soul. He was calling and seeking to inspire faith in the heart of this one destined to become the "father of the faithful."

How did God inspire such faith? It was:

I. *By means of a personal persuasion.*
  A. The personal name for God, Yahweh, was used (12:1).
    1. The unregenerate may speak of the Higher Power, Ultimate Cause, Original Force. So *Elohim* was often used.
    2. To Abram the *personal God* speaks personally (Hebrews 4:15).
    3. This name was first used by Eve (4:1), and then during the time of Enosh (4:26).
  B. The personal names of Abram and Sarai were used.
  C. Abram's personal circumstances were outlined.
    1. He was born in Ur of the Chaldees.
    2. Then he moved far away to Haran on the trade route.
    3. He faced the reality of death in the loss of a brother, Haran. (In Hebrew the man and the place are not the same.)
  D. Abram's personal responsibilities were described.
    1. Abram was not the oldest son, but he was second-in-command in Haran.
    2. Nahor, probably the oldest brother, was not present.
    3. The responsibility for about two thousand people fell on Abram at Terah's death.
  E. Even today God still speaks personally, not en masse (Psalm 139:1-4; Matthew 10:29-30).

II. *By means of a persistent persuasion* (12:1).

A. God's call to Abram came first in Ur and later was repeated in Haran (15:7; Acts 7:4).
B. Abram doubtless struggled with God's call for a considerable time before yielding.
C. God's call was a patient, persistent call to abandon every crutch.
1. To sever family ties.
2. To break political ties.
3. To discount economic ties.
4. To abandon personal ambition.
D. Only God's grace causes Him to repeat His call.
1. We must not presume upon it.
2. God may cease calling at any moment.

III. *By means of a purposeful persuasion* (12:1-3).
A. The divine command.
1. Expressed negatively, it was to turn his back on everything that had previously claimed his loyalty (repentance).
2. Expressed positively, it was to put God first in his allegience. (12:2d) (faith).
a. Man reaches his highest capacity for righteousness only through absolute commitment to God.
b. This commitment is expressed through faith toward God and the Lord Jesus Christ.
B. The divine purpose (12:2a, 2b).
1. To establish a great nation dependent on God's providence.
2. To bless Abram personally by achieving the highest possible development of his life.
3. God has purpose for every life even as He had for Abram.
C. The divine assurance. It would not be thwarted.
1. God's assistance was determined. (The use of cohortatives of determination indicated that His purposes would not be thwarted.)
a. God declared, "For I am *determined* to make thy name great."
b. God said, "The ones blessing thee I am *determined* to bless."
2. God's aid for His child may be anticipated.
3. Some feel they can't measure up to God's demands and thus refuse to accept Christ, but we have His wonderful assurance of His aid (Philippians 1:6).
D. The divine mission (12:2c, 3c).
1. God was and is engaged in reaching people for salvation.
2. Abram and all saved men are to be co-laborers with God in missionary and evangelistic endeavors.

Conclusion:
Man's response: Abram built an altar and worshiped.

13

The Tragedy of Forgetting God

Genesis 12:6–13:13

As I conducted revival services in the Vieux Carré of New Orleans, a young woman entered the auditorium one evening. Her make-up, clothes, and mannerisms suggested her particular occupation: a stripper and dancer in one of the many clubs on Bourbon Street. She had been born in a south Mississippi town. As a young teen-ager she had come to know Christ as her Saviour. For a while there was an altar in her heart, but she had forgotten God. Beginning to drift spiritually, time and depravity had pulled her down morally. By the time she was twenty-three, she was morally and spiritually bankrupt. But, she rebuilt an altar.

The experience of Abram anticipated the experience of many Christians. By faith Abram took that first step that crossed the mighty Euphrates and entered into a new life with God. Day by day God gave the orders that ultimately brought him to Canaan. One day God said, "This is the land," and Abram built an altar.

I. *The antidote to forgetting God–the building of an altar.*
  A. Abram's altar constantly reminded him of his utter dependence on God.
  B. Abram's altar testified to the vast differences between Abram and the Canaanites.
    1. The Canaanites were polytheistic and exceedingly immoral.
    2. Abram was monotheistic and ethical in dealing with others.
    3. The altar reminded him to be separate from the Canaanites and their sin.
  C. Abram's altar was associated with an increasing awareness of God.
    1. Abram's walk with God was by faith.
    2. God intensified Abram's faith by means of a theophany (12:7).
  D. Abram's altar encouraged an expanding comprehension of God's will.
    1. Abram probably went from Haran first to Damascus.
    2. Abram then journeyed to Canaan where God appeared and assured him about the land.
    3. Abram then built an altar as a part of his daily life.
  E. Abram's altar encouraged a growing sense of the real and permanent in contrast to that which is material and transient.
    1. He abandoned all that men count substance.
    2. Abram was seen "pitching his tent," but he was "*building* an altar."

II. *The possibility of forgetting God–the absence of an altar.*

A. Abram became engrossed in earning a living. (In a time of famine he naturally turned toward Egypt.)

1. God had not commanded Abram to do so. Thus it was not His will.
2. Abram apparently did not consult Him.

B. Abram was economically successful in Egypt.

C. But, Abram was spiritually a failure in Egypt.

1. He built no altar in Egypt as a testimony to his faith.
2. He had no time for God.
3. He failed to trust God for his protection.

D. Previous spiritual victories do not keep one from being a target of Satan. For example:

1. Moses, at Kadesh smiting the rock (Numbers 20).
2. Elijah, after his encounter with Ahab at Mt. Carmel (I Kings 19).
3. Jesus, in the wilderness after His baptism (Matthew 4:1-11).

III. *The tragedy of forgetting God–the lack of the godly influence of an altar.*

A. Abram compromised the truth and lived a half-truth. (This may have been a regular policy for him at this time.)

B. Abram became a curse to his associates rather than a blessing (12:17).

C. Abram lost his positive influence for righteousness over Egypt. The "salt had lost its savor" and was cast out.

D. Then Abram returned to the altar that he had originally built and unto God.

E. But Abram's influence on others was jeopardized, e.g., on Lot and his family.

1. The possibility of strife was acknowledged.
2. The separation between them was widened.

14

The Specter of War

Genesis 14:1-24

The drums of war were beating loudly. The flags of nations and the standards of allied troops were flying at the head of marching columns of soldiers. Black clouds of war were hanging low, while conflicts seemingly reached worldwide proportions and engulfed the nations of Abram's day. Abram and Lot were caught in the midst of it.

Since that day God's people have repeatedly been involved in the conflict of opposing forces as wars have raged over land, power, and wealth. The scourge of war was very real to the people of Israel. The sound of invading Syrians raised fear in many hearts. The onslaught of the ferocious Chaldeans made such an indelible impression on the minds of the people of Jeremiah's day that the word *Babylon* became a reminder of terrible judgment.

In successive order Israel faced the invading armies of the Egyptians with their armed chariots, the Assyrians with their battering rams, the Babylonians with their ravaging hordes, the Greeks with their implements of siege, and the Romans with their fearsome phalanx.

In Europe the invading hordes of Goths, Gauls, and Visigoths brought terror and death. In more recent days the armies of Napoleon scourged the earth. The Little Corporal claimed that God is always on the side of the strongest battalions. But his superior forces could not withstand the allied troops under Wellington at Waterloo.

Our own land has felt the pain of war in the Revolution, War of 1812, Mexican War, and in the agonizing conflict of the Civil War which pitted brother against brother. China, Japan, and India also suffered the scourge of ancient warfare.

In 1914 the world fought the "war to end wars," World War I. Less than twenty-five years later the entire world suffered World War II, a war that surpassed all others in its destructive force. Surely, men hoped, that would be the end of wars, but since that day there has been almost constant conflict breaking out around the world.

Abram and his family were engaged in a similar outbreak. As they faced what to them was an international conflict, we note:

I. *The curse of war.*
   A. Begun by godless forces.
      1. The participants: both the oppressed and the oppressors.
         a. The lesser powers in the area of the Dead Sea refused to continue paying tribute.
         b. The major world forces to the north and east of Canaan sought to enforce a system of tribute.

2. The purpose: self-glory, material gain, and power.

B. Expressed by senseless fighting.

1. Persons: killing, maiming, terrorizing, raping, enslaving.
2. Property: plundered, squandered, razed, and destroyed.

C. Evokes meaningful faith. Men frequently call on God during conflict. (Chaplain Fullilove wrote of the Vietnam war, "Where is God in all this?")

1. War may be a rod of punishment to the rebellious. It should have warned Sodom.
2. War may be a staff of chastisement for God's children.
   a. Often it is a means used to lead us to consecrate ourselves to God.
      (1) War makes praying amazingly meaningful. (Lot was probably praying as he had not prayed for a long time.)
      (2) Prayer time is not reckoned wasted time in combat. (As a Civil War chaplain told his troops: "Pray and keep your powder dry.")
   b. Often it is an opportunity to demonstrate to the world how to suffer.
3. War was a challenge to Abram's faith in God's providential care.

II. *The courage of love.*

A. Abram, the Hebrew ("the one crossing over"), was notified expeditiously by an escapee.

1. All Christians have "crossed over" from death to life.
   a. There is a point of crossing.
   b. They become a new creation in Christ Jesus.
2. All Christians should appear as a foreigner, i.e., a pilgrim, to others because he has "crossed over."
   a. Abram had a higher kingdom citizenship than that of this world.
   b. Abram had a higher allegiance that led the survivor to inform him.

B. Abram was concerned for Lot as his spiritual heir of the covenant.

C. Abram acted courageously, utterly dependent upon God.

1. He gathered 318 soldiers from his own men who could bear a sword.
2. He pursued the larger army and attacked surprisingly by night. (The speed of Abram's pursuit and the surprise of a night attack were in Abram's favor.)
3. He liberated the captives and reclaimed the spoils.
4. His love provided the courage that was needed.
5. He refused to count the cost or consequences because of his love for Lot.

III. *The consequence of faith.*

A. A royal convocation: three heads of state.
  1. King of Sodom.
  2. Priest-King of Salem, Melchizedek.
  3. God's ambassador, Abram.
B. A rewarding demonstration: the giving of tithes to Melchizedek.
  1. It expressed Abram's gratitude. Thus tithing is based on love and not law.
  2. It demonstrated Abram's faith. This was utter dependence on God.
  3. God responded later by promising to bless (15:1). You can't outgive God.
C. A righteous condemnation.
  1. The king of Sodom schemingly sought to obligate Abram.
  2. Abram expressed a godly denunciation of Sodom's king by the oath, "I lift my hand."
  3. Abram absolutely refused to compromise with Sodom.
  4. Abram resolutely set his faith in God, and in Him alone.

Conclusion:

All the while Abram had his eyes on Lot. He was concerned for him and the people of Sodom. Our concern for others should lead us to live and act as Abram did in peace or in war.

15

The God Who Quiets All Fears

Genesis 15

Fear is one of the most paralyzing, demoralizing factors experienced by man. Man may strive to appear foolhardy, but his fear is nonetheless real, for all his bravado. The only lasting answer to such fear is faith in Christ. For example, think of the death of five young missionaries at the hands of the Auca Indians of Equador. They knew that they were in a place of danger, but they felt definitely that the place where they were was the place that God would have them. They faced death unafraid.

The setting for Genesis 15 is plainly the episode of the preceding chapter that brought fear to Abram. God dealt with His follower to alleviate his fears.

I. *The answer to fear: faith.*

A. Fear was very real and apparently well-founded to Abram.

1. He feared the cruel reprisal of Chedolaomer and other kings of the East.

a. Abram did not possess sufficient men to repel an entire army.

b. The invading kings would be looking for this new adversary.

2. He feared the evident prospect of being without a child as an heir of the Covenant.

a. Lot seemingly had been accepted as an heir by Abram, but not by God. (Lot had compromised himself by living in Sodom.)

b. Abram's chief servant, Eliezer of Damascus, apparently was his legal heir. (Abram wondered if this was God's intention.)

3. He feared the manifest possibility of failure to possess the Promised Land.

a. The Amorites, an awesome and numerous people, populated the land in Abram's day.

b. Abram did not understand how he could achieve its possession.

B. Faith in the Lord God was the remedy for every fear to Abram.

1. The use of the term *Lord (Adonai),* signifying Master, is a meaningful recognition of the sovereignty of God. (Some interpreters charge that the names of God are used indiscriminately in this passage.)

2. Fear of reprisal had paralyzed Abram, childlessness had discouraged him, and failure to possess the land led him to despair and anxiety.

3. Then God appeared with the command: "Fear not . . ."; and a promise: "I am thy. . . ," (15:1).
   a. Shield—protection. (Precaution without Providence is vain. Amos described such a one as running from a bear only to be bitten by a serpent.)
   b. Reward—recompense. "Though I gain the world and have not Jesus. . . .")
4. Abram believed, or literally, "leaned on Yahweh."
   a. He who wavered was made stable by Him on whom he leaned. As we trust in Him we begin to share His character.
   b. He who wondered was made righteous by Him on whom he trusted.
   c. "What a fellowship, what a joy divine, leaning . . ." (song by Elisha A. Hoffman).

C. Faith in God yet remains the divine remedy for man's fears.
   1. We have fear of the natural and unnatural, known and unknown, life and death, age and disease, pain and daily needs.
   2. We have a satisfying recourse in faith. God is still our Shield and Reward.

II. *The reward of faith: a covenant relationship.*

A. The covenant conditions.
   1. On man's part faith was demanded (commitment).
   2. On God's part truthfulness and lovingkindness (*chesed*) was assured.

B. The covenant blessings (15:6).
   1. Righteousness is imparted to every sinner who responds by faith.
      a. It was given to Abram as imputed righteousness.
      b. It is given to all who trust God. (I saw a seventy-three-year-old man experience this righteousness by trusting the Lord. We could say, "He doesn't deserve it." But neither do I.)
   2. Judgment falls on all persons who rebel (15:16).

C. The covenant promises.
   1. God would make Abram's descendants as the stars of the sky (15:5).
      a. In an earlier day men may have scoffed at this. One could not see very many stars with the naked eye.
      b. But since Galileo's discovery of the telescope, they appear almost infinite.
   2. God would provide discipline in discipleship (15:13).
   3. God would give Abram's descendants a promised land of approximately 300,000 square miles (15:18). (Presently Israel is only about 7,800 square miles.)
   4. God promises to give Himself. There is no greater gift.
      a. Jesus offers to all men the New Covenant.
      b. He has sealed it with His own blood.
      c. Those who know Him in it need have no fears.

16

The All-Seeing Eye of God

Genesis 16

Barbara Gaultney wrote:

> I've seen it in the lightning,
> Heard it in the thunder,
> And felt it in the rain;
> My Lord is near me all the time.

She was very much aware that our God is One who both hears and sees us at all times.

With keen interest I examined a U-2 plane which had been used for high-level surveillance in espionage work. Underneath the plane I saw a small crystal dome approximately three inches in diameter through which a camera's lens was directed. At sixty thousand feet nothing of consequence could escape the camera. Even minute objects could be enlarged upon development.

Even more so we cannot escape the all-seeing eye and the all-hearing ear of God. He sees and knows and acts in behalf of those who are His children.

I. *God sees man's frustration* (16:2, 4, 7-8).
  A. Frustration had been produced by impatience.
    1. Impatient because of the failure of normal means in producing an heir to the covenant promises.
      a. Due to their ages Abram (85) and Sarai (75) feared that they were beyond their normal capacity for producing an heir.
      b. Due to the passing of a complete decade without the fulfillment of the covenant promise about an heir, they felt they needed to improvise alternate ways for producing a child.
    2. Impatient because of the failure of alternate legal means in producing an heir.
      a. Abram contemplated his chief steward, Eliezer, as a logical possible heir.
      b. Sarai considered her handmaid, Hagar, as a legal possibility to produce an heir.
      c. God rejected both of these timely possibilities.
    3. Impatient, as we often become, of having to "wait on the Lord."
  B. Frustration had been produced by impertinence.
    1. Impertinent in assuming God's role in fulfilling the covenant.
    2. Impertinent in "improving" on God's work in fulfilling the covenant. (In reality they were running ahead of God.)

3. Impertinent in accepting polygamy in fulfilling the covenant. (Its failure increased their frustration.)

C. Frustration is produced today by our inadequacies.

1. Unsuccessful in our aspirations (e.g., "Peace now" goal is so elusive).
2. Dissatisfied with our achievements.
3. Inadequate to solve our perplexing problems.

II. *God sees man's separation* (16:4-6).

A. His separation resulting in discord in man's marital relationships. (The harmony of a happy home life gave way to the discord of disagreements.)

1. Abram and Sarai were divided. Sarai blamed Abram for her predicament.
2. Sarai and Hagar were divided. Hagar held Sarai in disdain.
3. Abram and Hagar were divided. Abram failed in his responsibility to Hagar.

B. His separation resulting in stress on his spiritual relationships. (Man and God become estranged when man is separated from his fellowman.)

C. His separation resulting from sin. (Man's alienation is caused by his rebellion against God.)

1. Social divisions exist throughout the world due to sin.
   a. Ideological divisions. (Communists attempt to exploit basic separation between the proletariat [working class] and the bourgeoise [middle and ruling class].)
   b. Racial divisions. (Race is set against race.)
   c. National divisions. (Nation is set against nation.)
2. Spiritual separation from God is evident throughout the world due to sin.
   a. Through the use of L.S.D. and other hallucinogenic drugs.
   b. Through the fashion trends that encourage immodesty.
   c. Through increasing social consumption of alcohol.
   d. Through the presence of corruption in government (the Watergate Affair).

III. *God sees man's efforts at self-salvation* (Galatians 4:22-28).

A. Self-salvation by "improving" on God's divine work of salvation.

1. The promised seed seemed so slow in coming.
2. Thus they proposed a salvation by works through Ishmael.

B. Self-salvation by designing an impotent salvation by works.

C. Self-salvation that decrees Christ plus something else, rather than Christ only.

1. Salvation by church membership.
2. Salvation through the sacraments.
3. Salvation by good works.
4. Salvation through education.
5. Salvation through financial accumulation.

IV. *God sees His plan of salvation perfected with determination.*

A. In fulfillment of His promises.

1. His covenant was still to be fulfilled through a promised son of Sarai and Abram.
2. His covenant was ever to provide salvation by faith.

B. In the lives of His people.

1. In Hagar and Ishmael whom He preserved from disaster.
2. In Abram and Sarai whom He prepared for fuller service.
3. In the lives of those today who turn to Him through Christ His Son.

17

The Sufficiency of God

Genesis 17

We live in an age in which many people doubt the sufficiency of God. We have become so accustomed to having all the details of our lives worked out in advance, all our plans made for years to come, and all our necessary provisions for the future stored back that we seldom know the delight and joy that comes from depending upon the sufficiency of God. Abram's age was similar to this age. It was no easier for him to trust God completely than it is for us. But the Father of the Faithful, the Friend of God, was learning to trust God through each experience of his life.

Can God be trusted today? For over six years I felt that I should enter graduate school. However, when the time came, I knew no way to continue. No grants were available to me. I promised the Lord, however, that I would continue until He closed the door. Shortly after that I was requested by a professor, with whom I had had no previous relationship, to serve as his fellow. On the last day that I had to make the final decision, it appeared as though God had closed the door. By midafternoon I concluded that I could no longer continue my program of training. Within an hour God opened the door in two more marvelous ways: a teaching position in my chosen field of study at Union Theological Seminary in New Orleans and a property grant of rent from my uncle and aunt, Mr. and Mrs. Francis Amy. God still meets all our needs and is to be trusted in this day! He is a God who is sufficient.

We often think that Abram's life was one continuous experience of seeing God. That is not so. We find that only at crucial times in Abram's life did God appear. For example, when Abram arrived in the land at seventy-five years of age; again when he feared reprisal from the kings of the East; and when he was ninety-nine years old and yet no son (heir) had been born. The covenant God, Yahweh, came to reveal His sufficiency to Abram.

God was:

I. *Sufficient to institute the covenant* (17:2).

- A. By choosing Abram to institute the covenant with him. (This is election.)
  1. This covenant *(berith)* was based on Yahweh's lovingkindness *(chesed).*
  2. A covenant is an agreement or relationship between two or more persons.
- B. By promising Abram to provide for the present and eternity. (This assures ultimate perfection.)

1. Abram was called to give up his land; God promised to give him a new land.
2. Abram was called to forsake his kindred according to the flesh; God promised to give him a son and a great family.
3. Abram was called to renounce his worldly birthright; God promised to bless and make *Abraham* a blessing (17:5, 8).

C. By eliciting from Abram a proper response.
1. Faith—"Be thou *perfect*" (17:1). The emphasis of this word is on one's attitude. (It is better to strive for such a high goal than to be satisfied with attaining a lower one.)
2. Obedience—"Walk before me." This means to be conscious of God's standard and to live according to it.

D. By calling men today to enter the New Covenant through Christ.
1. God is sufficient to establish this relationship (Ephesians 2:8-9).
2. He calls men to Himself though we are all sinners (Ephesians 2:1).
3. He has taken the initiative and elected us. He said, "Ye have not chosen me, but I have chosen you" (John 15:16).

II. *Sufficient to sustain the covenant relationship.*

A. By revealing Himself as *El-Shaddai* to give assurance of His ability (17:1).
1. The term *El* is reflective of power.
2. The term *Shaddai* is indicative of His sufficiency, or dependability. ("Almighty" fails to convey this meaning.)

B. By providing the rite of circumcision to remind them of this relationship (17:10).

C. By changing their names to encourage them.
1. Abram was changed to Abraham ("Father of a Multitude").
2. Sari was changed to Sarah ("Princess").
3. Sinners when converted are called *saints*.

D. By rejecting Ishmael to indicate divine determination to provide the promised heir (17:17-21).
1. Abraham would have been satisfied with the second best.
2. Ishmael symbolized man's futile efforts at saving himself.
3. God often takes from us that which pleases us to give us something that is far better.

E. By working in the believer today to sustain the New Covenant (Philippians 2:12-16).

III. *Sufficient to consummate the covenant relationship.*

A. By multiplying Abraham's descendants.

B. By making Abraham the father of many nations.

C. By developing Abraham's spiritual maturity in the promises.

D. By consummating the New Covenant through the redemptive work of Christ. What man cannot possibly do for himself, God does (Philippians 1:6; Hebrews 12:1-2).

18

The Prayer of a Righteous Man

Genesis 18

In James 5:16 we read, "The effectual fervent prayer of a righteous man availeth much." In Abraham we see personified the blessings issuing from the prayer of a righteous man.

Prayer has been described in a multitude of ways:

"Prayer is the slender nerve that moves the omnipotence of God."

"Prayer is laying hold of the power of God."

"Prayer is man's extremity crying out for God's sufficiency."

"Prayer is an effective catapult activating God's intervention."

"Through prayer our source of divine grace is supplied and sustained."

Men have testified to the power of prayer in their lives:

Billy Graham begins no crusade without months and years being spent first in prayer for God's blessing.

Charles Spurgeon of London, when asked about his effectiveness in the pulpit, spoke of the "power room" under his pulpit where his deacons prayed as he preached.

Martin Luther said, "If I have a Christian who prays to God for me I will be of good courage, and be afraid of nothing."

Mary, Queen of Scots, said of the mighty Presbyterian preacher, "I fear the prayers of John Knox more than the armies of France."

God's Word pays tribute to the prayers of many a righteous man:

Paul and Silas prayed, and the windows and doors of a Philippian prison were opened through the moving of God.

The church prayed for Peter who was in a Jerusalem jail, and the chains fell loose and the doors opened to set him free.

Daniel prayed and the hungry lions of Babylon had an immediate case of lockjaw.

Hananiah, Mishael, and Azariah prayed, and they stepped forth from the Babylonian furnace that had destroyed those who cast them in it.

The young, righteous king Josiah prayed, and the hand of God's judgment on Judah was stayed for fifty years.

Isaiah prayed as the Assyrians besieged the city of Jerusalem, and 185,000 Assyrian soldiers were slain by the Angel of the Lord in one night.

Hezekiah prayed when God foretold his death, and fifteen years were added to his life.

Elijah prayed, and the heavens were stopped and rain came only when he prayed again to that end.

Joshua prayed and the walls of Jericho thundered to the ground.

Moses prayed for forgiveness in Israel's behalf saying, "and if not, blot me, I pray thee out of thy book which thou hast written," and he withstood the wrath of the God of Israel.

Abraham prayed, and God promised deliverance for Sodom and Gomorrah if only ten righteous souls could be found.

The prayer of a righteous man is:

I. *Based on a personal experience with God.*
   A. As evidenced in the visit of three angels with Abraham
      1. Abraham did not immediately identify them, though there was something strange and unusual about these heavenly visitors.
      2. Abraham exhibited a growing awareness of his visitors' position by his hospitality that far exceeded mere Oriental courtesy.
         a. Posture of humility (18:2).
         b. Politeness in approach (18:3).
         c. Preparation of a sumptuous meal (18:8).
         d. Prerogative of God recognized (18:10).
         e. Possession of divine knowledge realized (18:13).
         f. Providence of God considered (18:18).
         g. Purpose of God revealed (18:20-22).
   B. As evidenced in Abram's full surrender at Haran to follow by faith God's leading to an undesignated land.
      1. He had to turn his back on the world.
      2. He had to turn his face toward God (15:6).
   C. As evidenced in the conversion of one willing to follow Christ by faith.
      1. His justification is assured as he prays, "God, have mercy on me a sinner."
      2. His place in Paradise is assured by the prayer, "Lord, remember me when thou comest into thy kingdom."
      3. His power in prayer is assured by the promise that "if we ask anything according to his will, he heareth us."

II. *An avenue of divine blessings on others* (18:19).
   A. As demonstrated by the blessings upon Abraham's children and descendants through his prayers.
      1. Isaac and Ishmael were blessed through him.
      2. The children of godly parents who know how to pray for them are greatly blessed. (Such a blessing can be of far more value than an insurance policy.)

3. Wayward children have been reclaimed and have testified to the power of prayer upon them.

B. As demonstrated by the blessings upon Abraham's nephew, Lot, and the cities of Sodom and Gomorrah.

1. Lot and his immediate family were spared.
2. The cities would have been spared if only ten righteous men could have been found.

III. *An expression of deep compassion and concern* (18:23-33).

A. Abraham exercised intercession in prayer for Sodom, though the city was separated from him by a tremendous spiritual gulf.

B. Abraham evidenced a deep concern in prayer not only for Lot and the righteous ones, but for all. (Where could he have learned this but from God?)

1. Lot should have begun a "church" by then and led in bringing at least ten souls to the Lord out of Sodom.
2. Lot had back-slidden into spiritual stagnation and had not even "moved his church letter."
3. Lot was "vexed," but he had exerted precious little spiritual influence.

C. Abraham expressed boldness in prayer (18:27).

1. His prayer was not boastful, but humble ("dust and ashes").
2. His prayer was not demanding, but pleading.

D. Abraham exercised a persistence in prayer.

1. Basing his request upon the character of God (18:23).
2. Asking God to spare the city for fifty, forty-five, forty, thirty, twenty, and then ten righteous persons.

E. Abraham's experience in prayer needs to be exemplified in our lives today.

1. It will ultimately lead to blessings for others.
2. It will constantly be a means of blessing to us.

19

Lessons from Sodom
or
Take Heed, America!

Genesis 19:1-3, 12-29

Sodom with its environs was a showplace of the ancient Canaanite world. Teaming with wealth, prosperity, and superabundance, it was compared to "the garden of the Lord" (13:10).

Located in what is now the dry, salty, sulphurous area of the Dead Sea, the area was once rich in fertility and luxurious in green pastures. But prosperity and the goodness of God did not turn the inhabitants to righteousness. They grew worse and worse until the very name of their city became used to describe one of the grossest of human sins, sodomy.

In their day of peace, prosperity, and plenty, they felt that they could do as they pleased without retribution. No thought was given to the judgment of God. The order of the day was reveling, feasting, and satisfying the appetite of sensual lust.

But judgment had been decreed. The scales of God's justice were balanced with the sentence of utter destruction upon the cities of the plain. God's mercy and lovingkindness were long lasting, but to those who spurned His love it was not everlasting. The hounds of God's judgment may run slowly, but they run nonetheless according to the timed decree and severity of God's command.

From Genesis 19 let us note several lessons from Sodom:

I. *God's mercy provided an undeserved deliverance from Sodom* (19:1-16).
   A. Because Lot, with Abram, was a party to God's covenant.
   B. In spite of the fact that Lot pitched his tent *toward* Sodom.
      1. He began to walk in the counsel of the ungodly and to stand in the way of sinners.
      2. He sat in the gate of Sodom serving as a public official.
      3. He was found by the angelic visitors to be spiritually backslidden, though he was prosperous and politically powerful (19:1).
   C. In spite of Lot's spiritual compromise. (But he "vexed his righteous soul," II Peter 2:8.)
      1. He had won no one to a saving faith in God.
      2. He had not even won his children. (He could lead them into Sodom, but he could not lead them out.)
   D. In spite of the impending destruction.
      1. Lot was warned by the two angels for Abraham's sake.

2. His heart was filled with fear and terror.
3. He sought to warn his daughters and his prospective sons-in-law (19:14).
4. He failed to convince them of the impending destruction. (They considered him as one that mocked, i.e., a fool.)

E. By overcoming Lot's reluctance to leave the city.
1. The material things for which he had worked were difficult to leave behind.
2. The influential position of Lot made leaving most difficult.
3. The angels took Lot's hand and his wife and two daughters and led them out of the city in the darkness of early morning.

F. In spite of Abraham's heavy heart.
1. He observed the black smoke in the sky and doubtless felt that his prayer was useless.
2. He did not yet know that God had spared Lot and those who fled with him.

II. *God's wrath prompted a deserved destruction of Sodom.*
A. God's judgment was exercised because the city was past redemption. Its "cup of iniquity" was full.
1. It was a completely materialistic people.
2. It was a totally secular people.
a. They had no time for God.
b. They had no fear of God.
3. It was a singularly sensual and lustful people.
a. The attempted assault on the angels evidenced it.
b. The offer by Lot of his two daughters confirmed it.
c. The sin of incest between Lot and his daughters reflected it.

B. God's judgment brought total destruction to the cities and region.
1. The Great Ghore from Africa to Armenia probably shuddered.
2. The city began to quake and sink as the sun began to rise.
3. Faults and fissures began to split the earth.
4. Escaping gases began to explode, bitumen began to burn, sulphuric salts began erupting and raining back to earth.
5. Sensual women screamed, lustful men cursed, and terrified children cried.
6. Lot's wife tarried, looked back longingly, and was engulfed.
7. Abraham saw the black, rising smoke testifying to divine judgment (19:28).
8. The city disappeared from sight. (It is believed to be under the waters of the Dead Sea.)

III. *God's Word includes a warning declaration concerning Sodom* (II Peter 2:6).
A. To unrepentant sinners. (The plight of Lot's wife and Sodom is a divine warning of impending judgment).
1. That God's wrath is hot and His judgment is real.
2. That God's mercy must be sought while it is yet available.

B. To nations and peoples that forget God. (The plight of the "cities of the plain" is a warning to our nation today.)

1. Edward Gibbon in *The Decline and Fall of the Roman Empire* set forth four main reasons for the demise of the empire. Perhaps we need to look at our own nation for signs of decay.
2. Warning signs are up that should lead us to beware. America should take heed!
   a. Take heed, America, when the Great Society hopes to become rich by spending itself poor.
   b. Take heed, America, when a proposed cut in taxes is used as a launching pad for even higher taxes.
   c. Take heed, America, when one out of every three marriages ends in divorce and "no-fault divorce laws" scoff at divine standards.
   d. Take heed, America, when crime pays and accelerates at a rate surpassing that of population growth.
   e. Take heed, America, when the home of the brave has become the home of booze, housing a majority of the world's alcoholics.
   f. Take heed, America, when such a vacuum exists in the soul of your people that drugs become the way of turning on.
   g. Take heed, America, when pornography grips your inner cities and blights your villages.
   h. Take heed, America, when your theologians declare that "God is dead" rather than proclaiming the living God.
   i. Take heed, America, when your citizenry decrees by example that freedom of religion is really freedom from religion.
   j. Take heed, America, when your leading churchmen berate democracy but are silent regarding Communism's plan of world domination.
   k. Take heed, America, when one of your leading denominations encourages fraternizing with an enemy even at "the expense of national security."
   l. Take heed, America, when your moralists approve such pictures as "Who's Afraid of Virginia Woolfe" for home television in spite of its out-spoken profanity and specific vulgarity.
   m. Take heed, America, when your political leaders encourage anarchy and political espionage for personal advancement under the cover of "national security."
   n. Take heed, America, when your intellectuals preach an old immorality as the New Morality.
   o. Take heed, America, when your educational institutions restrict the devotional reading of the Bible, but offer courses in witchcraft and pagan religions.
   p. Take heed, America, when your courts enshroud the

Communist Party or any party with legality while it yet espouses the violent overthrow of this country.

q. Take heed, America, when you deny friends, but subsidize enemies.

r. Take heed, America, when respect for law degenerates until your police are viewed as villains and criminals as heroes.

s. Take heed, America, when nightclubs, dinner clubs, service stations, and movies employ undressed young women and increase their clientele.

t. Take heed, America, when homosexuality gains acceptability under the label of "gay" rather than being labeled as sick and corrupt.

u. Take heed, America, for when morals fall as did those of Sodom, nations fall. Righteousness still exalts a nation, but sin is a reproach to any people.

3. Billy Graham has said, "Unless God brings America to judgment, He should apologize to Sodom."
4. Such lessons must be learned before it is too late.

20

The Tragedy of Moral Relapse

Genesis 20

The Bible has much to say about lying and its consequences. Note some of the following verses:

> Leviticus 6:2-5; Psalm 31:18; 120:2-4; Proverbs 6:16-17; 21:6; Isaiah 57:11; Jeremiah 9:3, 5; Hosea 4:1; Zephaniah 3:13; John 8:44; Ephesians 4:25; Colossians 3:9; Revelation 21:8, 27.

Who would have thought that Abraham, the Friend of God, would have stooped to common lying in order to assure his own well-being? He, who only recently had interceded for the cities of Sodom and Gomorrah, now needed intercession for himself. He who had climbed high up the steep mountain of moral perfection had not reached the summit. He still faced sheer cliffs that brought terror to his soul.

Once before in Egypt Abraham had practiced the same deception, and had been rebuked by Pharaoh. Since that day he had lived nearly twenty five years in Canaan. He had been blessed by the Lord. On at least four occasions he had received the promise from God of a son by Sarah. From this son was ultimately to come the Saviour of the world. Abraham had liberated Lot from Chedorlaomer's captivity, repudiated the materialistic and immoral standards of Sodom, talked face to face with the Angel of the Lord, and yet he fell victim to the sin of deception for a second time.

In this chapter we see:

I. *The temptation of human desperation (20:1-2).*
  - A. In Abraham's moving his tribe to a dangerous area, the Negeb, south of modern Gaza.
    1. A drought may have caused the move in search of pasture.
    2. The destruction of Sodom may have led him to move.
    3. The presence of a strong Philistine population in Gerar endangered Abraham in this move.
  - B. In Abraham's fearing for his life.
    1. He did not know how he would be received.
    2. He did know that Sarah was an unusually attractive woman.
  - C. In Abraham's deception for the sake of expediency.
    1. He declared that Sarah was a half-sister. This was true (20:12).
    2. He neglected to reveal that Sarah was his wife. This made it a half-truth, or, "a little white lie."
    3. He committed a former sin that he had failed to forsake.
    4. He failed to rise to the challenge of the occasion.

II. *The conviction of divine revelation (20:3-8).*

II. *A sin-offering cannot be substituted by man.*

A. The necessary offering had been specified. (Man cannot barter with God.)

1. Men have tried to substitute many things: wealth, works, religion (Psalm 49:6-8).
2. Isaac recognized that though their hands were full, they did not have that which was required.

B. The sacrifice was to be spotless, pure, and unblemished.

1. The life of an unblemished animal was usually offered.
2. The life of a pure, spotless animal represented an offering of the best to God.
3. The lives of Isaac and Abraham required an acceptable offering because they were sinners.

III. *A sin-offering may be provided by God.*

A. This was Abraham's hope (22:5).

1. Abraham used three verbs to describe what he *and* Isaac would do: go, worship, and return.
2. These are verbs of determination that express his confidence.

B. This was Isaac's hope (22:9).

1. Isaac was a young man who could doubtless not be overpowered physically by Abraham.
2. Isaac chose to cooperate with his father in doing as God directed.

C. This was God's response.

1. God provided the necessary sacrifice, a substitute.
2. Abraham accepted the substitute by faith.
   a. In his heart he had surrendered everything, even Isaac.
   b. In his heart he accepted the ram as a true substitute to express the giving of self.
3. God accepted the offering, and Abraham.

IV. *A sin-offering is required even today.*

A. Just as Isaac and Abraham, we have nothing acceptable to offer a righteous God.

B. Just as God provided the ram as a substitute, He provided the sacrifice of His Son as our Substitute.

1. The sacrifice of Isaac in Abraham's heart anticipated God's offering of His Son (John 3:16).
2. The sacrifice of Christ is sufficient for eternity (Hebrews 9:28).

23

Walking Through the Valley of the Shadow

Genesis 23; Psalm 23:4

What would be your reaction to the death of a loved one? One young mother in New Orleans lost her four-year-old daughter, and she was bitter and rebellious against God. After burying her little girl, she remembered her daughter's recent words when she had saved some grapes for her: "The best for you, Mommy." Then on her knees she was able to say, "The best for you, God."

Everybody must, sooner or later, walk through the lonesome valley of the shadow of death. How comforting, how consoling, how encouraging it is to know the loving presence of our heavenly Father and Shepherd!

I have helped bury an infant that died at birth, and felt the pangs of sorrow with parents whose expended love was unreturned. I have buried the youth who died while yet strength and vigor surged in his body, and wept with parents who suddenly experienced the sorrow of dashed hopes and dreams. I have stood behind the caskets of young mothers and fathers, and shared the bewilderment of children and the loneliness of the grief-stricken mate who wondered, "What are we going to do?" I have also led the funeral procession into the cemetery as loving hands of friends and family serving as pallbearers have gently born the body of an aged father or mother to the grave, and thanked God for the years of a godly example and the influence of such a life. Each time I have been keenly aware that this experience, sooner or later, will be known by everyone.

What are we to do? Is there no help for one in the face of such an experience? The answer comes confidently and comfortingly: "Thy rod and thy staff, they comfort me." Abraham already had leaned on the Lord (Genesis 15:6), and leaning on Him he found comfort and help in the valley. Let us consider his experience in the death of his beloved wife, Sarah.

I. *Death is a universal experience of men.*
  A. Death comes to mankind without respect of persons except for two notable exceptions.
    1. Enoch who walked with God.
    2. Elijah who was carried away in a whirlwind.
  B. Death, that journey from whence no traveler has returned save Christ and those whom God raised from the dead, comes to even the faithful and beloved.
    1. Sarah, the heartbeat, the beloved, the adored of Abraham was not spared.
    2. Sarah, the wife who trod the Promised Land with Abraham for sixty-two years, departed in death.

3. Sarah, the only woman in the Bible whose age is given, died.

C. Death comes suddenly without a promise of another day.

1. Though men feel that they have a ninety-nine year lease on life, note the young men whose lives are cut off.
2. Though we hate to face it, the obituary columns list the young as well as the aged.
3. Consequently, we should live every day as though it may be our last.

D. Death finalizes man's opportunity to prepare for eternity.

1. An abundance of training materials are offered people to prepare them physically and materially for life.
2. A scarcity of training materials are provided for spiritual preparation for death.
3. No preparation for eternity is possible after the moment of death.
   a. Embalming and cosmetics are used to make one look natural, to camouflage the ravages of death, but these efforts are effective for only a short time.
   b. Cemeteries are called "Memorial Gardens," but they are graveyards reminding man of his need for spiritual preparation for eternity.

E. Death came even to Sarah, Abraham's beloved.

1. Abraham purchased the cave of Machpelah from Ephron for a burial place.
2. Abraham deposited the earthly remains of his wife in it.

II. *Death is a sad experience for men* (23:21).

A. Family relationships are brought to an end by death.

1. So the husband-wife relationship of Abraham and Sarah was ended.
2. So the mother-child relationship of Sarah and Isaac was ended.
3. So all family relationships are finalized by death.
   a. In heaven we will know one another.
   b. In heaven we will have an altered relationship.
   c. In heaven all will be children of the Father.

B. Business and social relationships are terminated by death.

C. Broken relationships bring sorrow without hope to many persons.

1. No rock is available to which one may cling.
2. No future is anticipated save an eternity without God.
3. To die thus without Jesus leaves no hope, regardless of the size of the monument that marks one's grave.

III. *Death, our enemy, can be met confidently and defeated.*

A. The Holy Spirit's presence, our Paraclete, is assured us.

B. Eternal reunion with our loved ones is promised.

1. Heaven is made more dear to us by our loved ones who are already there.
2. Our sorrow and loss should be seen as gain to those who are there.

C. Our ultimate victory is assured by Christ's resurrection (I Corinthians 15:55-57).

24

The Heavenly Matchmaker

Genesis 24:1-60

A foundation stone of society is the home. The most influential factor in the life of a person is the home. No wonder God places such responsibility upon parenthood that he would not and did not leave us without guidance upon such an important matter. We are not left merely to grope in the dark.

Associated with the home are the popular themes of love, courtship, and marriage. God does care about the love life of His children, but so often we reject so much of His care, we look so little for His leadership.

This matter about which we frivolously joke is of tremendous importance. In southern California one out of every two marriages is ending in divorce. Sociologists and psychologists as well as ministers are deeply concerned over the breakdown of homelife. When one out of three marriages are breaking up, what is the Christian answer? We need to hear God's Word in this aspect of life.

I. *The Lord leads those who will let Him lead in selecting a mate.*
   A. He led Abraham to certain convictions about marriage (24:3-4).
   B. He led Eliezer to the proper bride for Isaac (24:7, 14). ("His angel" was God's personal representative.)
      1. Marriages are made in heaven, but are wrought out on earth.
      2. God gives us all the parts, but success in marriage is a "do-it-yourself" project.
      3. Many who refuse to be led find marriage "a hell on earth."
   C. He persuaded Rebekah's parents to permit a marriage (24:50-51).
      1. These were believers. They held to high spiritual principles.
      2. They recognized his references to the Lord.
      3. Consideration of family background was important. (You better be sure you can get along with your mother-in-law. She may come to live with you, or you may have to live with her!)
   D. He convinced Rebekah to agree to marriage (24:57-58).
      1. She was a fellow believer. Why did Abraham insist that she not be a Canaanite? (24:3).
      2. She accepted God's will for her in regard to marriage (II Corinthians 6:14).
         a. A young wife who was married to an unbeliever said, "I love my husband. He is good to me and my children, but if I had it to do over, I would not marry him."
         b. Too many are like the girl praying about marrying Bill: "Lord, I want to do your will, just so long as I get my Bill."

c. It is important to put your best foot forward; but it is more important to let Christ lead.

II. *The Lord blesses those whom He leads together in marriage.* (The Western world follows the policy of falling in love and marrying. The Eastern world follows the policy of marrying and falling in love. They have fewer divorces.)

A. The Lord made a "love match" (24:61-67).

B. The Lord was placed at the center of the home from the beginning.

1. That is His rightful place in all our homes.

2. A judge advised, "You need a third person in your home."

C. The Lord brought comfort and joy into their lives.

1. Husbands are instructed to love their wives as Christ loved the church (Ephesians 5:25).

2. Wives are told to obey their husbands (Ephesians 5:22-24).

3. Fathers are to guide, but not provoke their children (Ephesians 6:4).

III. *The Lord inspires and strengthens His follower who is in a marriage with an unbeliever* (I Peter 3:1).

A. There may be heartache and adversity.

B. There can also be daily strength.

1. With determination to live a consistent, Christian witness.

2. With anticipation to win the unbelieving one to Christian faith. (A faithful Sunday school teacher prayed forty-five years for her husband who was finally converted.)

25

The Friend of God

Genesis 25:7-10; II Chronicles 20:7; Isaiah 41:8; James 2:23

The Bible magnifies the relationship of friendship in many ways. Great friends were David and Jonathan, Ruth and Naomi, Deborah and Barak, Elijah and Elisha, and Jeremiah and his scribe Baruch. Abiding friendships developed between Andrew and Peter, Paul and Timothy, Philemon and Onesimus, and John and Jesus. But nowhere does it call anyone other than Abraham "the friend of God."

In Genesis 25 we come to the conclusion of the Bible's historical record of Abraham. At the age of 175 years he found his life "full of years; and was gathered to his people." Through his experiences he became known as the friend of God.

Let us look briefly over his long life to determine how one becomes a friend of God. God's friend:

I. *Had a personal experience with God.*
   A. Abraham had the natural ambitions of wealth and personal power as a youth.
      1. Abram's fortune logically resided in Mesopotamia.
      2. But God asked him to turn his back on these things for Him.
      3. In the same way Christ called the "rich, young man" who, unlike Abram, refused to follow Him.
   B. Abram experienced the normal family ties of a young man.
      1. His father, Terah, was a pagan who worshiped the moon god.
      2. Abram doubtless was tempted to follow his father.
   C. Abram renounced the natural for the supernatural that he might follow and serve God.
      1. Family ties were broken. (A young woman followed Christ in baptism at Kaplan, Louisiana, though her parents tried desperately to get her to renounce her new faith; she insisted on following Jesus.)
      2. Social ties were broken. (Christ declared that we must be willing to forsake all for Him.)
      3. As Abram put God first he came to know Him personally.

II. *Placed his faith in God.*
   A. Faith in God became the primary expression of Abraham's life.
      1. In accepting the land, God said that it would be yet four hundred years before possession could be realized. This took faith!
      2. In anticipating a son, God withheld fulfilling this promise until Abraham was one hundred years old. This took faith!
      3. In acknowledging God's supremacy, God said to offer Isaac in sacrifice. This took faith!

1. In accepting the land, God said that it would be yet four hundred years before possession could be realized. This took faith!
2. In anticipating a son, God said that it would be when he was one hundred years old. This took faith!
3. In acknowledging God's supremacy, God said to offer Isaac in sacrifice. This took faith!

B. Faith in God was the stabilizing factor in his life.
1. The temptations of the world ever beckoned him.
a. On three occasions we see him fall: in Egypt, in Philistia, and with Hagar.
b. But faith, as a gigantic gyroscope, righted him.
2. His allegiance to God ever served as his guiding star.
a. At times he wandered astray.
b. This star brought him back.

C. Faith in the Lord led God to attribute righteousness to his life (15:6).
1. So "the just *shall live* by his faith" (Habakkuk 2:4).
2. So "by grace are ye saved through *faith*" (Ephesians 2:8).
3. So "God so loved the world . . . that whosoever *believeth* on him. . . " (John 3:16).

III. *Expressed his love for God.*
"A friend loveth at all times" (Proverbs 17:17).

A. In worship.
1. An altar located between Bethel and Ai was the focal point of his wanderings.
2. The altars of Abraham served as a lasting memorial that he had passed that way. (Abraham "built an altar" whereas Lot "pitched his tent.")
3. The altar on which Isaac was offered was the most sublime expression of worship.

B. In missionary efforts. "Be thou a blessing" (12:2).
1. He shared his faith with his household.
2. He witnessed against the sins of Sodom.

C. In loving obedience to the will of God.
1. The concrete evidence of love for God is faith *accompanied* by works.
a. Abraham rendered day-to-day obedience in the small things.
b. He also manifested obedience in the major commands to leave his family and to offer Isaac.
2. Jesus desires just such love today (John 14:15).

Conclusion:
You can be a friend of Christ today (John 15:15).

26

The Breakdown of a Home

Genesis 25:19-34

Here was a family divided. One member despised the other and not only refused to speak but also vowed to kill his brother. A preview of the coming disaster is indicated in the words, "thus Esau despised his birthright."

Family breakdown, tragedy, and breakup does not occur in just one day. Usually no one major act or deed is the culprit, but a persistent accumulation of small things until the breaking point is reached.

Let us see how it occurred in the family of Isaac and Rebekah. It happened:

I. *In spite of a good foundation.*
   A. Based upon the will of God.
      1. Abraham and Sarah led him to see the importance of the right spiritual choice.
      2. Eliezer prayed for the divine will as he sought a bride for Isaac.
      3. For forty years Isaac had waited for the right woman.
      4. You need patiently to seek His will concerning the prospect of marriage.
         a. A devout Christian who married rather late in life declared: "Some people fall in love, but we crawled." He meant that they had carefully sought God's will.
         b. Another such friend who married at age forty said: "Boy, it's the real thing." He meant that he had found joy in Christian marriage.
   B. Based upon prayer concerning the major issues of life.
      1. Isaac prayed about the lack of a child.
         a. Twenty years later his wife bore the coveted children.
         b. Their birth was a cause for joy.
      2. Rebekah prayed about her unusual condition in bearing twins.
      3. Prayer was apparently a normal experience for this home.
         a. Worship was not confined to the Sabbath. (Note their regular communion with God.)
         b. Prayer was not confined to emergencies.
         c. Every home needs such a wise foundation.

II. *Because of a foolish example* (25:28).
   A. An evident difference was noticeable in these two brothers.
      1. Esau: an outdoorsman.
         a. In appearance he was reddish, or ruddy, and hairy.
         b. In temperament he was impetuous, reckless, careless, and wild.

2. Jacob: a home boy, tied to his mother's "apron string."
   a. In appearance he was fair complexioned and had a smooth skin.
   b. In temperament he was deliberate, cautious, careful, restrained, and conscientious.

B. An evident partiality was shown by their parents.
   1. Isaac loved Esau, his opposite. Isaac was placid.
   2. Rebekah loved Jacob, her opposite. Rebekah was ambitious.
   3. Flagrant, evident partiality is a seed of family disaster.

C. An evident love for physical pleasures and temporal values was displayed by Isaac.
   1. Isaac placed a growing importance on personal pleasure.
      a. His appetite was a point of weakness.
      b. Esau developed a weakness also in his fleshy lusts.
   2. In many homes today young people are taught that the greatest values are physical ones.
      a. Girls are led to believe that physical beauty and social esteem are life's highest goal. They are encouraged, "Marry a rich husband."
      b. Boys are taught that life's greatest goal is the accumulation of wealth.
      c. Spiritual realities are reserved for life's emergencies, a sort of eternal fire insurance.

III. *Resulted in tragic consequences.*

A. Jacob felt free to take undue advantage of his brother.
   1. He knew Esau's weak spot and exploited it.
   2. He desired the birthright.
      a. Physical blessings in receiving a double portion.
      b. Special leadership in family affairs.
      c. Spiritual leadership in family worship.
   3. He sought it in the wrong way and had to flee.
   4. He refused to wait until God would work it out.

B. Rebekah deliberately planned to deceive her husband.

C. Esau sought to achieve material goals rather than spiritual ones.
   1. He put more value on his stomach than on his soul.
   2. He was alienated from his brother and parents.
   3. He contracted marriages with Canaanite women to spite his family (28:8-9).
   4. His life failed to bring glory to God.

D. Isaac failed to be as strong an influence for righteousness as Abraham had been or as Jacob would be.
   1. His position as leader of the faithful was compromised.
   2. Our lives, also, may be crippled and limited by such a family disaster.

27

The Fear of Isaac

Genesis 26:24-25, 34-35; 27:30-33; 31:53

If the name of a person is important to him, how much more important is a divine name. By a name a person is identified and remembered. In the age of the patriarchs, a name had unusual significance. It was a means of revealing one's self. By the knowledge of one's name a person had a degree of influence with him.

Throughout Genesis, we find a diversity of divine names. By this means God revealed more and more of Himself to His followers. For example in:

Genesis 5 - *The One True God* with whom Enoch and Noah walked in the midst of a corrupt, pagan world.

Genesis 14 - *El-elyon, God Most High* who rules by right of creation.

Genesis 16 - *El-roi, the God who Sees,* the One who sees and knows our needs.

Genesis 17 - *El-shaddai, the All-Sufficient God* who is adequate to meet our needs.

Genesis 18 - *Lord, the Master* who is sovereign over His followers.

Genesis 21 - *El-'olam, the God of Eternity* who rules through the ages.

Genesis 22 - *Yahweh-yireh, The LORD who Provides,* who provides our sacrifice.

Genesis 24 - *The Yahweh God of Abraham* who leads through *the Angel.*

It would seem that here are sufficient names for a great and glorious God. But there is yet another name. Growing out of the events recorded in Genesis 26–27 is the name Jacob used to describe God. He called Him the *Fear of Isaac.*

Isaac has been described as the ordinary son of an extraordinary father, and the ordinary father of an extraordinary son. But his life reveals forcefully that "God rules in the affairs of men."

We note that:

I. *The Fear of Isaac made Isaac tremble greatly* (27:33).

A. Though Isaac possessed several commendable qualities.

1. Isaac was the chosen recipient of the covenant promises (26:3).
2. Isaac followed God's leading in his life (26:2, 6).
3. Isaac determined in his easy-going way to live at peace (26:20-22).

4. Isaac received many blessings from God (26:29).

B. Because Isaac was spiritually insensitive in regard to Esau.

1. As revealed in his refusal to accept God's choice of Jacob over Esau.

a. He failed to learn of such choices from Abram.

b. He failed to note its similarity to God's choice of him over Ishmael.

2. As manifested in his failure to magnify spiritual values as greater than physical and material ones.

3. As indicated in his determination that his elder son, Esau, would receive the blessing.

C. Because Isaac was providentially overruled by God.

1. A new spiritual perception caused Isaac to tremble. (It was not age or illness.)

2. A new willingness to acknowledge that such a covenant blessing for Esau was completely out of God's will made Isaac to tremble.

II. *The Fear of Isaac led Isaac to submit to His will.*

A. By recognizing and accepting the divine revelation concerning Jacob and Esau (25:23).

B. By recognizing and acknowledging the dominant worldliness in Esau's life.

1. Esau's selling his birthright indicated it. (He was more concerned with his stomach than with his soul.)

2. Esau's marriage to two Hittite wives confirmed it (26:34-35).

3. Esau's refusal to accept the consequences of his earlier decision reflected it (27:34-36).

4. Esau's characterization as a "profane man" reflected it (Hebrews 12:16).

C. By recognizing and admitting that Jacob truly hungered for spiritual things.

1. Yahweh had originally prophesied it.

2. Isaac ignored it and gave Jacob little nurturing in the fear and admonition of the Lord.

3. Rebekah unwisely guided Jacob's basic desires and led him to employ the wrong means to achieve the right end.

4. Isaac recognized God's providential intervention in his dealings with Jacob and Esau, and trembled at the prospect of circumventing God's will.

III. *The Fear of Isaac led Jacob to serve Him.*

A. By exerting a continuing influence on Jacob.

B. By exercising a continuous protection of Jacob.

1. In protecting him from Laban.

2. In bringing him safely to Canaan.

Conclusion:

God still rules over the affairs of men. He will rule in your life, or be

1. An acceptance of God's provisions (28:20).
2. A surrender of life's ambition. Now he yielded to God's way.
3. An expression of constant devotion (28:22b).
4. A promise of faithful stewardship (28:22c).

D. Reveals to us our need for such a memorial.
1. In a personal conversion experience.
2. In the realization that our body is the Holy Spirit's temple.
3. In our love for God's house. (Such love will express itself in reverence and faithful support.)

II. *The Memorial at Mahanaim: God's Host* (31:44 f; 32:1 f.).

A. Communicated Jacob's grave peril.
1. Due to his misplaced trust in himself. (He was still growing spiritually.)
2. Due to the hasty pursuit of Laban and his sons.
3. Due to Laban's ability to force Jacob's return to Haran.
4. Due to Jacob's lack of a strong fighting force.
5. Due to Laban's search for the teraphim. (Rachel had taken it because its ownership enhanced one's claim as a true heir.)

B. Commemorated God's adequate protection.
1. As seen in His quieting the wrath of Laban (31:24).
2. As seen in Laban's report that encouraged Jacob to greater trust (31:29).
3. As seen in the sealing of a covenant of peace between Jacob and Laban.
4. As seen in the presence of God's Host who was ready to help.

C. Conveys man's need for true spiritual perception.
1. In our own day.
   a. As Jacob's eyes were open to see God's providential care.
   b. As Elisha's servant's eyes were open to see God's protection.
   c. As the three Hebrew children's confidence in facing the furnace.
2. For the future. (God's Host yet protects us, Acts 12:7; Hebrews 1:14).

III. *The Memorial at Peniel: God's Face* (32:30).

A. Signified the estrangement between Jacob and Esau.
1. As Jacob depended upon self to effect reconciliation.
2. As Jacob depended upon bribes to placate Esau (32:13-20).
3. As Jacob depended upon luck to overcome Esau (32:7-8).
4. As Jacob depended upon these, he found that they failed to satisfy.

B. Signified the solution to Jacob's predicament which was to trust God completely.
1. Jacob separated himself for prayer (32:22-24).
2. Jacob came to the place of dependence upon God (32:26).
3. Jacob's name was changed to Israel (32:28).

4. Jacob then met Esau in joy and confidence (32:30).

C. Symbolizes the need for such a memorial in our lives.
   1. As we come to depend solely upon God.
   2. As we come to enjoy daily His favor and fellowship.
   3. As we come to solve our problems through His presence.
   4. As we come to experience fully the joy and contentment of living daily before His face.

30

Some Modern Motives for Tithing

Genesis 28:20-22

A dedicated Christian entered a new occupation. While I was visiting in his place of business, he asked that we pray and dedicate it to God. After I prayed, he did, and said, "Lord, as you bless me I will use this business to bless you." In his company's charter he stipulated that 10 percent would go for God's work through his church. In spite of stiff competition and discouragement, I saw his tithe increase steadily. His business continued to grow. As God has honored him, he has continued faithfully to honor God with his tithe.

A Department of Internal Revenue agent was questioning a man about his income tax return. He said, "Sir, you indicate that you gave 10 percent to your church. Nobody gives that much. Can you verify it?" He wondered what would lead a person to do that. He did not see how he could do it, and he wondered why others would do so. The man being questioned was able to bear witness to his love for Christ and used the incident to invite the agent to attend church the next Sunday with him.

It is often said, "I wonder what makes him tick?" This means what factors motivate that person. As a mainspring is to a watch, so is a Christian's motives to his work, witness, and worship.

Motivation is important in all that we do, but especially so in giving. A one-million-dollar ring from a wealthy tycoon may be lightly handled as a child's plaything, while a bouquet of bitterweed blooms from a chubby hand may bring tears to a mother's eyes. The difference is motivation.

In the Bethel experience, Jacob was not bargaining with God. Instead of fear, he now possessed faith; instead of despair, hope; instead of darkness, light; instead of anxiety, peace. Consequently, he was expressing his gratitude to God.

Many people today, like Jacob, have committed themselves to the practice of tithing. Several motives mingled together enforce their commitment.

Let us look at some of these modern motives.

I. *To receive the material blessings God has promised to the tither* (Malachi 3:10).
   A. Some may never get beyond this step. It is a beginning, but it is selfish.
      1. If this is the basic reason for tithing, a person may not continue to give very long.
      2. God's blessings frequently take forms other than material.
   B. Many tithing testimonies bear witness to material gains (e.g., a

dedicated mobile-home dealer told of a phenomenal economic growth that accompanied his commitment to tithe).

1. When using 9/10 as God wills, it usually goes further than 10/10 spent without regard to God's desire for us.
2. To rob God is to rob self. It is usually true that either willingly or unwillingly we tithe.

II. *To take advantage of the tax structure.*

A. Our government recognizes the importance of charitable contributions by permitting certain percentages of one's income to be exempt from taxation. (Ten percent has been the normal amount permitted, but tax advantages may be enjoyed by giving even larger amounts.)

1. These gifts may have to be verified. (One person called his church office wanting the church office to verify a 10 percent contribution, though he gave practically nothing. Not only did he lie and steal; he wanted the church to do so also.)
2. These tax advantages may be removed by the government at any time.

B. Our concern with this motive should apply only to gifts above the tithe recognizing God's claim upon it regardless of any tax advantage.

III. *To acknowledge God's ultimate ownership* (Psalm 24:1).

A. Tithing recognizes that the good earth belongs to God.
B. Tithing expresses our stewardship of His resources.

IV. *To develop a deeper faith.*

A. In the promises of God's Word.
B. In the providences of God to provide all our needs.
C. In the power of God.

1. To deliver us from the sin of covetousness.
2. To enable us to overcome the temptation of materialism.
3. To defeat our tendency to live self-sufficiently. (Many persons have given the tithe which at that time was all that they had, but God provided for their personal needs.)

V. *To invest in Kingdom-building enterprises.*

A. By engaging in the church's worldwide task of evangelism through giving.
B. By implementing God's plan of tithing that He gave to support such a task.

1. Not by raffles and bingo games.
2. Not by ice cream suppers or chicken suppers. (Churches that need to depend upon such plans to support its work may be as cold as the ice cream and as dead as the chicken.)

C. By sharing in a missionary-oriented unified budget and the Cooperative Program.

1. To meet the local needs of a church's ministry.

2. To reach out to the needs in countries from Afghanistan to Zambia.
3. To participate in a many-faceted ministry of teaching a man to read, healing a sick girl, or leading a boy to Jesus.
4. To "hold the rope" for missionaries by meeting their needs.

VI. *To express gratitude and love for Christ*. (This is the highest motive.)

A. As Jacob expressed his gratitude and love for God by his vow to tithe.
1. Ingratitude is a deplorable vice in anyone (e.g., a father worked to send his son to college, but the son, upon graduation, was ashamed of him and refused to speak to him).
2. Gratitude was a commendable virtue in Jacob's response.

B. Because God expressed His love for us by giving His best, His Son.

C. Because true love finds expression in sacrificial giving.
1. Jesus demonstrated that "it is more blessed to give. . . ."
2. We respond and find it to be true as we faithfully trust Him with the tithe.

31

When God Is Near

Genesis 29:1–30

When the Christ child was born in Bethlehem, the wise men of the East saw His star and set out to find, adore, and worship the One "born King of the Jews." In Genesis 29, we find Jacob, just as surely under the leadership of God, making a similar journey in the opposite direction. Along this way Abraham had traveled. Eliezer had gone this way seeking a wife for Isaac. Now Jacob travels the same path. The Hebrew may be translated, "Then Jacob began to lift up his feet and came. . . ." Here is a figurative picture of a journey, "picking them up and putting them down." It was not a leisurely pace, but a journey being made with deliberate speed.

Jacob had recently met the Lord and had come to know Him personally. As he traveled the approximately five hundred miles, his new faith in God bade farewell to his old fears. Whereas Jacob apparently had been making the journey all alone, now he was keenly aware that another One walked beside him. He became conscious of, and committed himself to, the leadership of Yahweh God. Even so, we can know the presence of the Lord with us. We, too, can know His leadership.

Note that, when God is near:

I. *There is direction in life* (29:1).
   A. Man has a natural desire for purpose and direction to life.
      1. Many men look to the wrong source for direction.
         a. Many "causes" become a consuming passion temporarily.
         b. Many "causes" fail to bless others or bring personal satisfaction.
            (1) Consider the example of Solomon (e.g., constructing beautiful buildings, designing a world empire, fostering alliances with foreign nations, acquiring great knowledge, amassing a personal fortune, marrying many wives, and having pleasure ever at his command).
            (2) Consider the conclusion of Solomon concerning it: *vanity*.
      2. Many fail to find a sense of direction.
         a. Consider the derelicts and addicts who are stumbling down blind alleys.
         b. Consider the suicides who are seeking escape from unbearable realities.
            (1) It is an admission of man's failure to conquer "inner space" at a time of the conquest of outer space.

(2) It is the second-leading cause of teen-age deaths.
(3) It has been the escape for several notable entertainers and celebrities.
(4) It has been the end of people who are financially successful.
(5) It testifies that direction cannot be found in things.

B. Jacob found the direction he desired for life in God.
   1. He surrendered himself to God—the right person.
   2. He sought to serve God with his life—the right plan.

II. *There is leadership in life's decisions.*
   A. Divine leading in one's decision regarding marriage. (Next to one's salvation, this is the most important decision.)
      1. Desirous of privacy for his first meeting with Rachel, Jacob requested the shepherds to leave and return to the pastures (29:7).
      2. Delighted at the sight of Rachel, Jacob kissed her, and wept! (29:10-11). (It was love at first sight.)
         a. Such conduct indicated his tenderness and susceptibility to spiritual affairs.
         b. Such conduct introduced him as a benefactor rather than a suppliant.
         c. Such conduct indicated his competitive spirit. (He was able to do alone that for which the shepherds were waiting for more help, 29:10.)
      3. Disappointed by his marriage to Leah, Jacob continued to love Rachel.
         a. Laban deceived him (29:23).
         b. Jacob still was able to marry Rachel (29:30).
   B. Divine leading in one's decision regarding his life's vocation.
      1. Jacob was led in accepting wages for his work as a shepherd (30:43).
      2. He was led later to return to his own land (31:3).
   C. Divine leading in all of life's decisions.
      1. It is the Christian's greatest joy to be and to do what God desires for him.
      2. It is available to those who singularly desire it.

III. *There is peace in the midst of life's tempests.*
   A. The life of God's man is not free from tension and trials.
      1. Such as in the deception of Laban.
         a. Toward Jacob's marital plans.
         b. Toward Jacob's wages.
      2. Such as in the hostility of Jacob's brothers-in-law (31:1).
      3. Such as in the hatred of Esau.
   B. The life of God's man is marked by peace and serenity.
      1. God's promised presence was an assurance of providential care.

2. God's work was to take present disappointments and make them future blessings.
   a. Such a promise is ever certain (Romans 8:28).
   b. God will not stop His work in us until it is complete (Philippians 1:6).

32

Human Channels of Divine Blessings

Genesis 30:25-31, 43 (or 29:31–30:43)

Jacob was the recipient of the covenant promises that had been made to Abraham. God had said, "For I am determined to bless you." He had assured Jacob's fearful heart at Bethel that He would bring about his return to the land. At Bethel Jacob met the Lord and seemingly came to know Him in a meaningful experience of salvation. From that moment he knew the assurance of God's blessings in his life. He became a human channel of divine blessings.

Such persons:

I. *Recognize that God is the origin of all blessings*. "Every good gift and . . ." (James 1:17).

A. God grants spiritual gifts which are of eternal significance.

1. Salvation, including the past, present, and future, is the primary blessing.

a. It is adequate to live by.

(1) It was for Adoniram Judson preaching seven years in Burma without a convert, even facing imprisonment.

(2) It was for William Carey going to India as the first representative of the modern missionary movement.

(3) It was for John Bunyan suffering imprisonment in the Bedford jail for preaching the gospel.

(4) It was for David Brainerd living and serving in the wilderness with the Indians until his health broke.

b. It is sufficient to die by. (Materialism fails; science fails; the god of pleasure fails.)

(1) It was for Bill Wallace who stayed at his post in China until he was imprisoned and tortured to death.

(2) It was for Jim Carlson who stayed at his post in the Congo until he was massacred.

(3) It was for my pastor-friend Aaron Trahan who, at the age of twenty-nine, faced death as the portal to heaven.

2. Preservation in the God-called, God-oriented life is a resultant blessing.

a. Jacob had a natural tendency to backslide.

b. God continually drew him back (cf. Philippians 1:6).

B. God gives physical gifts which are of temporal significance.

1. Jacob's children were recognized as gifts from God (29:32, 33, 35; 30:6, 18, 20).

a. Children are to be received as a divine heritage (Psalm 127:3).

    b. Children should be received with gratitude.
  2. Jacob's wealth was seen as a gift of God (31:42).
    a. God gives the ability to get wealth (Deuteronomy 8:18).
    b. God promises an adequate amount (Psalm 37:25; Matthew 6:33).
    c. This gift has the potential of becoming a snare as it did to Jacob.
  3. Jacob's blessings at times appeared in disguise.
    a. Laban's deceit: Jacob became wealthy in spite of it.
    b. Crippled by the Angel: Jacob developed spiritual maturity in spite of it.
    c. Bitter and grievous events: God worked it for good in spite of them. (An experience with an ulcer while I was in seminary conveyed lasting truths about the futility of excessive anxiety.)

II. *Enrich the lives of those associated with them.*
  A. Laban was blessed for Jacob's sake (30:27).
  B. Lot was blessed for Abraham's sake (8:23–19:20).
  C. Pharaoh and Egypt were blessed for Jacob's sake.
  D. Others are to be blessed for our sake.
    1. "Salt" is not to be saved, but to be used. Then it blesses.
    2. "Light" is not to be subdued, but to shine. Then it blesses.

III. *Realize that God's blessings are to be used to serve God.* (The greatest enjoyment of any blessing is to use it to its maximum for God; to be a channel, and not a reservoir, of blessings.)
  A. Through the child that God gave.
    1. Is he considered to be insurance against your old age?
    2. Or is he an investment in God's worldwide kingdom?
    3. Have you truly offered him or her to God?
  B. By means of the wealth that God gave.
    1. Do you use it singularly for self?
    2. Do you use it for the Saviour? (Dr. N. S. Cutrer was an outstanding dentist who could have become wealthy, but he chose to use his dental skills to bless God. He invested in missions by personally purchasing needed items for missionaries to use in numerous parts of the world.)
  C. With the personality that God gave.
    1. It may be utilized for self.
    2. It should be invested for God to bless Him.

As Jacob, we should become human channels of divine blessings.

33

God Leads His Dear Children Along

Genesis 31:1-7, 19-25, 41-42

The headlines read, "Mother Shoots Daughters and Husband." The story related that a woman had taken a rifle and shot her children while they slept and her husband when he returned from work. She said, "God told me to do it." Does God lead His children like that?

The headlines read, "Man Slays Son." The story related that a father took his son out one night, tied his hands behind his back, placed his body on a make-shift altar, and thrust a knife into his son's heart. He explained, "God told me to sacrifice my son to him." Does God lead His children like that?

A missionary was warned of impending danger at his post of service and was encouraged to leave. Feeling that it was God's will that he remain, he stayed and met death at the hands of savages. Does God lead His children like that?

A young man had built a successful contracting company in the building industry. Feeling God's call to missions, he became a foreign missionary helping to build needed church buildings. Lady Fortune and her companions whom he forsook will never be his in this world. Does God lead His children like that?

Many are asking, "How does God lead a person? How can I know His will for me?" Jacob experienced this in his life. We see the answer in Genesis 31 as God leads His dear children along.

God leads in the doing of His will:

I. *By an inward desire.*
   A. Jacob had an inward desire for spiritual things.
      1. It led him to seek Esau's birthright in return for a bowl of red soup.
      2. It prompted him to deceive his father in securing the desired blessing of the "double portion" and leadership in spiritual matters.
      3. The methods used were despicable and indefensible, but his motive was right.
   B. Jacob had a deep desire to return to his country.
      1. He had previously indicated it to Laban (30:25).
      2. God's promises to him were associated with the land.
   C. One's deepest desires may be a divine impression of God's leading.
      1. A Levite's service in the ministry was a result of desire (Deuteronomy 18:6-7).

2. Paul's efforts at evangelism among his people were a result of desire (Romans 10:1).
3. Paul's work in Rome was a result of a great desire of many years (Romans 15:23).
4. William Carey desired to see the heathen converted, and it led him to India as a pioneer of the modern missionary movement.
5. Charles Whitefield desired to burn out for God, and he became a flaming firebrand in England and America.
6. D. L. Moody desired to be the one man totally dedicated to God, and he moved America and England closer to God.
7. Baker J. Cauthen desired to lead souls to Christ, and it led him to China and to the Foreign Mission Board of the Southern Baptist Convention as Executive-Secretary.
8. We are directed to desire specific things.
   a. The office of a bishop (I Timothy 3:1).
   b. Spiritual gifts (I Corinthians 14:1).
   c. The sincere milk of the Word (I Peter 2:2).

II. *By the spoken word.*
   A. God affirmed Jacob's desire with the explicit word (31:3).
   B. God may speak audibly, or through His written Word, the Bible.
      1. He spoke to the vile heart of Augustine, *"Tolle, lege; tolle, lege."* This means "Take and read; take and read." He picked up the Bible and read Romans 13:13-14 and was converted.
      2. He spoke to Martin Luther on the steps of *Santa Scalla* in Rome. The words of Romans 1:17 kept ringing in his ears.
      3. He spoke to John Wesley in Aldersgate in London, and his heart was "strangely warmed."
   C. God's Word is to determine our conduct and actions.
      1. According to the example of Christ.
      2. According to the spirit of Christ. (A young minister spoke bitterly of his call to "fight" within the church. His attitude was foreign to the spirit of Christ.)

III. *By His providential provisions and protection.*
   A. In Jacob's daily experiences.
      1. His wives acquiesced in leaving their father (31:14, 16b).
         a. When one's wife is willing to go wherever He leads, he has a great blessing.
         b. When one's family is unwilling to go wherever He bids, he has a great handicap. (Many men whom God has called to His ministry have been stymied at this very point.)
      2. God blessed in the accumulation of sufficient provisions (31:9).
      3. God protected him against Laban (31:24, 42).
      4. God led Jacob to be sure that going back to Canaan was the divine will.
   B. In the daily affairs of men (Romans 8:28).
      1. As seen in past history. (Man proposes, but it is God that

disposes. Man does not make history; God makes history. Man records it.)

a. Gideon "put out the fleece." At times we must do so.
b. William Carey intended to go to Burma, but God closed the door to Burma and opened the door to India.
c. Judson and Rice intended to go to India, but God sent Judson to India and Luther Rice back to the United States.
d. An older minister friend of my father would have had to drop out of Acadia Baptist Academy where he prepared himself to preach except for two boxes of groceries providentially provided by a church at a time of critical need.

2. As realized in present experiences.

34

A Spiritual Struggle in the Night

Genesis 32:21-31

A lovely child was born into a king's palace. Every possible opportunity for greatness and usefulness belonged to this child. Wealth, education, power, and popularity were his. But God smote the child with a strange illness. Physicians were consulted, but they could do nothing to alter the course of the illness. The father, the king, lay down in the dust and prayed for seven days. He refused to eat or to be consoled. He besought the Lord, but the child died. When he learned of the child's death, his first act was to go to God's house for worship. This experience helped make David one of Israel's greatest kings. Certainly David never forgot his struggles through the darkness of those nights.

I had talked to a man about his eternal salvation. Late into the night I assured him that, if he would surrender and accept Christ, the Lord would forgive him. About midnight I left him in a state of indecision and rebelliousness. Through the night he tossed and tumbled and thought. In the early hours, his wife awoke as he got out of bed and began to dress. He said, "I am going to kill that preacher and then kill myself." His wife jumped up and begged him to trust the Lord; she assured him that his problems could be solved in the Lord. And there in those early hours he gave his heart to Jesus. He never forgot that struggle in the night.

A young couple had drifted far away from God. At one time they seemingly loved Him and served Him. But then they began to be interested in other things. They found nightclubs and dances more attractive than God's house. They began to spend their money and God's money on alcohol. Then one night their little daughter became violently ill. A physician was called, and, after his examination, he said that it was beyond a doctor's hands. At 4:00 A.M. the pastor was called. He went to the house to pray. The father said, "Wait, I can't pray." He went to the kitchen, emptied his bottles of whiskey, and then they prayed. By 6:00 A.M. the doctor said, "The child seems to be coming through." Those parents never forgot that struggle through the night. Many victories are still won by such struggles.

Jacob is a worthy example of this truth as he struggled. His struggle was:

I. *Required because of Jacob's false dependence on himself.* (He felt adequate and sufficient.)

  A. Trusting in his winsome personality (32:3-5).

    1. He sent messengers to prepare Esau.

    2. He magnified Esau's position. (Note Jacob's use of "my lord Esau; thy servant Jacob.")

3. He suppressed the idea that he had returned to claim his inheritance (32:5).
4. One young man who trusted himself admitted that he had entered the ministry on the basis on his own personality. He soon failed.

B. Trusting in his luck, or good fortune (32:6-8).
1. Hoping that at least one group would escape, Jacob divided his family and belongings into two groups.
a. No child of God should permit "blind fate" to hold a controlling interest in his life.
b. It is not luck, but God's love that blesses the life of Christ's disciple.
2. Failing to be sufficiently satisfied, Jacob began to pray (32:9-12).
a. His endeavor in prayer was proper, but it was limited.
b. He still felt that success depended primarily on him.
c. He failed to surrender himself fully, for fear still held sway.

C. He trusted in material wealth and bribery (32:13-21).
1. Five different gifts at intervals were designed for their psychological impact on Esau.
2. Psychology, as a substitute for spiritual experience, is never sufficient.
3. Jacob discovered that he could know very little peace through depending upon his wealth.

II. *Required to lead Jacob to a more complete trust in God.*

A. Rest would not come. His fear was very real.
1. Jacob was staying with his family, but he felt that human resources were inadequate.
2. Jacob moved them in the night across the Jabbok (32:22).
3. He then drew alone to seek a solution to his predicament.

B. God came to draw Jacob completely to Himself.
1. A man appeared in the night. Later He was revealed to be the Angel, God incarnate.
a. No luck was possible. Suddenly the man was upon him.
b. No bribes were available. That was across the ford.
c. No personal strength was left. Jacob was wounded.
d. Then he perceived the divine qualities about this man.
2. Jacob recognized the man as the Angel, or Yahweh's personal representative (32:26).
a. God changed Jacob's name from Jacob, "Supplanter," to Israel, "God's Prince," or "He who Strives with God."[1]
b. Jacob asked about God's name, i.e., His character. This was growth in grace.
c. In a time of crisis at my daughter's birth, my prayer moved

[1]Cf., Derek Kidner, *Genesis: an Introduction and Commentary*, p. 170.

from an expression of selfishness to total surrender of her to God. That was growth in grace.

C. Jacob's submission to God brought him to a new standing with God.
   1. God's presence was evidently shining in him as Jacob limped across the Jabbok in the early sunlight.
   2. God's strength was evidently sufficient for him as Jacob faced the prospect of meeting Esau with the assurance of success.

35

The Reality of Forgiveness

Genesis 33:1-11

Separating many a man from where he is spiritually and where he ought to be is a grudge, or an unforgiving spirit. One day as I talked to a man who had drifted away from God, he told me that sixteen years previously he had been wronged. Through misrepresentation and dishonesty he was injured deeply. For sixteen years, he had borne the ravaging fire of an unforgiving spirit within his bosom. It had eaten at his soul day and night as a spiritual cancer. He had been the loser for it.

Jacob had been separated from the Promised Land because of malice, hatred, and an unforgiving spirit. When he had left, Esau had sworn unswerving vengeance for the wrongs that he had sustained at Jacob's hands. He threatened to kill him at the earliest opportunity. But God had said to return. God was not content with his child being in the far-off country of Padan Aram. He wanted Jacob back in the Promised Land. But first Jacob had to forgive Esau, realize God's forgiveness of himself, and secure forgiveness from Esau. Such could not be done without God's help.

A forgiving spirit:

I. *Is necessary for God's child.*
  A. Jacob had become keenly aware of this personal need in regard to Esau.
    1. It was a constant shadow over him in Haran.
    2. It was a burning issue in his night struggle with the Angel.
    3. It was uppermost in his mind as he prepared to face Esau directly.
      a. He divided his family into three divisions: handmaids and their children, Leah and her children, and Rachel and little Joseph.
      b. He took the lead position personally.
    4. It led him to cleanse his own heart in confession and now to seek reconciliation.
  B. Jacob had openly acknowledged his need of, and desire for, forgiveness (Genesis 32:3-5).
  C. Every Christian needs to give and to seek forgiveness for wrongs committed.
    1. An unforgiving spirit is evidence of a lack of divine forgiveness (Mark 11:25-26; Matthew 18:35; James 2:13).
      a. "One who is unforgiving is unforgiven because he is unforgivable," according to Frank Stagg.

b. Unforgiveness is an able deterrent to Christian growth.

2. A forgiving spirit reflects our forgiveness by God.

a. Of Henry VI of England it was said: "He never forgot anything but injuries."

b. Of Cranmer, Archbishop of Canterbury, it was said: "If you want to get a favor from him, do him a wrong."

c. Of Lincoln, Emerson said, "His heart was as great as the world, but there was no room in it to hold the memory of a wrong."

d. C. H. Spurgeon said, "Pray for a short memory to all unkindness."

II. *Includes making amends for wrongs* (33:8).

A. By making restitution.

1. Previously Jacob had deceptively achieved the blessing.

2. Now Jacob was offering abundant gifts in return.

3. Later the Law specifically required this.

B. By righting wrongs against others where possible.

1. Forgiveness is not to be cheapened by merely saying, perhaps with a grudge, "I'm sorry."

2. Forgiveness is likely to be costly. (The Internal Revenue Service received a check for a wrong return with interest from a man who said, "I have become a Christian . . . and wish to make this right." It cost him.)

C. By understanding the Biblical concept of forgiveness.

1. Three Hebrew words which mean forgiveness.

a. "Cover"—*Capār*—used two times.

b. "Lift up"—*Nasa*—used sixteen times.

c. "Send away"—*Salāh*—used thirty-three times.

2. Three Greek words which mean forgiveness.

a. "Loose away"—*appolúo*—used two times.

b. "Be gracious to"—*charizomai*—used fifteen times.

c. "Send away"—*aphéame*—used fifty-two times. (Primarily this reflects God's act.)

3. The Christian's translation of forgiveness is to "be gracious" toward others (Ephesians 4:32; Colossians 3:13).

III. *Is realized through God's help* (33:5, 10-11).

A. In Jacob's experience.

1. God used chastisement to bring Jacob to seek forgiveness.

a. Homesickness.

b. Estrangement.

c. Insecurity.

2. God used an expanding awareness to lead Jacob to see that "vengeance is the Lord's."

a. Through protection from Laban.

b. By means of the watchcare of God's Hosts.

B. In Esau's experience his heart was divinely touched and led to respond to Jacob.

C. In the present-day Christian's experience.
   1. We are to recognize our example in Christ who forgave those who crucified Him.
   2. We are to realize that we have been forgiven for so much: all of our sins.
   3. We are to reflect God's presence within us by forgiveness.
      a. E.g., over a period of time a personal experience with unforgiveness brought despair, uselessness, and hopelessness until it was settled in prayer in the dark hours of one morning.
      b. E.g., two shopkeepers fell out with one another. After four years one went to apologize and led the other man to Christ.

36

When Sinners Talk Like Saints, and Saints Live Like Sinners

Genesis 34:1-5, 25-31

The Bible is no mere book of hero worship. If it were, this sordid event in the lives of Jacob, his sons, and Dinah would have been struck from the record. But the Bible deals with the real issues of life—real "flesh and blood problems" that confront man and can only be overcome through the power of God.

Jacob had promised Esau to visit him in Seir. He felt, however, that his family would be safer in Shechem, so he purchased a field there. He built an altar and worshiped God there. But he still tolerated idolatry and sin in the lives of his family.

Jacob went to visit his aged father, Isaac, from either Succoth or Shechem. Deborah, the nurse of his deceased mother, returned with him. Surely he found some comfort in Deborah's accounts about the final years of his mother's life.

Possibly eight of nine years had elapsed since Jacob had left Padan Aram. Dinah was about six years old when her father settled in Succoth. At the time of the account in Genesis 34, she was around fifteen or sixteen years old. On a visit with the girls of Shechem, she was led away and sexually assaulted by an older young man. In trying to make amends for his sinful deed, the young man, Shechem, asked for permission to marry Dinah.

In the ensuing events we see that sinners at times can talk like saints, and saints can often live like sinners:

I. *As evident in Jacob's era.*
   A. Sinners could talk just like saints (34:20-24).
      1. They were willing to be circumcised, to "become Israelites," for social reasons (34:21).
      2. They were willing to become Israelites for material gain (34:23).
      3. They were willing to make amends after shamefully and flagrantly flaunting Dinah's personal rights for marital privileges.
   B. Saints could live like sinners.
      1. Jacob was guilty of being too permissive with his children, including Dinah and his sons.
         a. No words of rebuke or correction are recorded prior to these events.
         b. No positive and effective witness is evident in Jacob's life during this period.
      2. Dinah was possibly guilty of impropriety (34:3). Perhaps she shared in the guilt.

a. In her visiting such a group alone.
b. In her failure to struggle or resist.
c. In the possibility of her encouragement of the affair.

3. Simeon and Levi were guilty of mass slaughter.
   a. There was no excuse for their deed. Jacob never approved it (cf. 49:5-7).
   b. They made the innocent suffer along with the guilty.
   c. They masked their vile deed with the cloak of religion!
4. Jacob's other sons (we don't know if they *all* did, or not) shared in the plundering (34:27).
   a. They excused it as righteous indignation (34:31). (It is never righteous when such deeds are expressed in an unrighteous manner.)
   b. They could rationalize their plunder by the fact that it was convenient.

II. *As evident in the Calvary events* (II Corinthians 5:21). (What an awesome miscarriage of justice!)
  A. The crucifiers felt just like saints.
    1. They were only doing what was necessary, for their welfare!
    2. They proclaimed Christ's guilt and their innocence, because, after all, He was the one being crucified.
    3. They asserted their willingness to believe, if only He would come down from the cross.
  B. The disciples who were saints lived like sinners.
    1. In that Simon cursed and denied Him. He has many descendants today.
    2. In that His disciples forsook Him and hid in fear.
    3. In that the Crucified who *became* sin for us was left alone.
      a. His was a tremendous load to bear: the sins of the world.
      b. His pure mind in which an evil thought never originated or found harbor, His heart which never contemplated any lustful deed, His body that never performed an evil act—became sin!

III. *As evident in our day.*
  A. Frequently sinners talk like saints.
    1. Politicians use the Bible and religion for personal gain.
    2. A tavern keeper placed a sign on his door saying, "Go to church Sunday."
    3. The businessman speaks of civic righteousness, but lives a degraded life.
  B. And saints live like sinners.
    1. Its evidence is seen in many expressions.
      a. In a sub-Christian social life that is scarcely different from that of an unbeliever.
      b. In a permissiveness towards one's family responsibilities.
        (1) Even today many children are given the heavy responsibility of telling their parents what to do.

(2) "In the modern home everything is run by switches except the children."

c. In a preoccupation with sexuality that leads to immorality.
   (1) Faced on magazine racks.
   (2) Seen repeatedly on television.
   (3) Accepted by some as a normal expression of life (cf. Galatians 5:19-21).

d. In the reflection of hatred, jealousy, prejudice, and pride in one's life.

2. Its presence has produced several results.
   a. Doubts regarding one's experience of salvation. (Many persons have asked, "Pastor, if I'm saved why have I done this?")
   b. Lack of ability to bear one's witness to the world.
   c. Lack of power to live a victorious, Christian life.

3. It needs to be dealt with specifically.
   a. Through confession.
   b. By repentance.
   c. For restoration. (It is possible for those who desire it (cf. I John 1:9).

37

The Necessity of Spiritual Renewal

Genesis 35:1-10, 15, 19-20, 22, 28-29

Thirty-five years had passed since Jacob had been at Bethel. On that eventful night he had seen his destitute condition. He also saw God's might and power to provide his needs, and there surrendered himself to God. There "he found the Lord," or really, was found by the Lord, and went forth in the power of His might. It would be wonderful to say, "And it was all well ever after," but it does not work that way spiritually.

Jacob's life was a series of mountaintop and valley experiences. He was first up and then down. His spiritual life may well have been compared to a modern roller coaster. There were high spiritual ecstasies followed by moral depression. He was often "down." God's man may be down, however, but he is not to be "down and out."

In Jacob's experience of going back to Bethel, we see:

I. *Crises that call us back to Bethel.*
   A. Deaths. (These may bring personal crises.)
      1. Favored Deborah died (35:8).
      2. Beloved Rachel died (35:19).
      3. Jacob's father, Isaac, died (35:29).
   B. Disappointments.
      1. Jacob's children did not measure up to his life (35:22).
      2. Jacob's brother gave no assistance.
   C. Discouragements.
   D. Diversionary tactics of Satan.
      1. Leading us to be preoccupied with material goods and feeling self-sufficient. (Jacob had become quite wealthy.)
      2. Encouraging us to satisfy our fleshly appetites.
         a. With sexual immorality (34:1 ff.). (Rather than drawing us closer to God as it was intended in its holy expression, its exploitation erects a barrier between us.)
         b. With uncontrolled anger, wrath, and vengeance. (Some say, "I just speak what I feel," but so does a child or an ignoramous!)
      3. Diverting our attention to less important matters.
         a. Such as Jacob's responsibility of directing a large family.
         b. Such as becoming involved in so much that is incidental that it conflicts with our paramount loyalty.
   E. Decisive call of God.
      1. One's original Bethel experience when God speaks spiritual life to his soul is a glorious experience.

a. It was for me. (The Lord saved me in Orange, Texas, in 1939. In 1957 I went back, and though the church building was gone, I located the very place that it had occurred. I rejoiced in the memory of that event.)

b. It was for you. (Do you recall it?)

2. Passing years may have brought strange gods to infect our lives, but God can tolerate no other gods.

a. Our love becomes strained, artificial, and unreal (Revelation 2:4).

b. Dissatisfaction and unhappiness are used by God to call us back.

3. God's Spirit arrests us, convicts us, and calls us back to Bethel.

II. *Factors that need renewal in a Bethel experience.*

A. An adequate prayer life (35:1). An "altar" was a place of prayer.

1. To recognize God's sovereignty and adequacy.

2. To acknowledge our submission to God.

3. To become prayer warriors; not silent tin soldiers. (At one time you may have prayed as a skilled musician plays a mighty organ with its many stops, but now it is more like the sound of cotton balls falling on a carpeted floor. We need prayer warriors; not silent tin soldiers.)

B. A life of purity (35:2).

1. In speech.

a. E.g., Joseph Valachi, a former member of the Mafia, learned a new vocabulary in order to testify of crime's infiltration of America.

b. E.g., note the difference between the "sanitized" public statements of former President Nixon and the gutter language of personal conversation as revealed in the Watergate tapes. (What if God released His tapes on you?)

2. In conduct.

C. A commitment to personal witnessing (35:5).

1. We must speak of the "terror of God."

2. We must tell of the love of God. (We sing, "I love to tell the story,"[2] but are silent. Then tell it!)

D. A life dedicated to faithful service (35:1).

1. Recognizing Sunday as the Lord's Day. (We inform new Christians that Sunday is the Lord's Day, but they see many Christians who treat it as though it belonged to them.)

2. Glorifying the Lord every day.

3. Participating in the regular services of our church.

a. New Christians are usually informed that they need both services on Sunday and one on Wednesday to help them live for Christ through the week, but they see so many who do not practice it.

[2]Song by Katherine Hankey.

b. Good habits are learned and enforced by good examples.

E. A life committed to faithful stewardship (28:22).
  1. Jacob had been prosperous, but then permitted problems to arise.
  2. Jacob had been successful, but then God put a ‘‘limp’’ in his leg.
    a. Like Jacob we may have begun as good stewards, but have faltered by the wayside.
    b. Like Jacob we need to begin anew with God.

38

The Peril of Rejecting God

Genesis 36:1-2a, 6-8

As a young man sat on his tractor one day, I talked to him about his spiritual needs. His godly mother was praying desperately for her son's salvation. He was healthy—the outdoor type who loved the woods. He was strong—his occupation as a logger developed bulging muscles. He was young—approaching his twenty-sixth birthday. But he was rejecting God! He was not openly rebellious. He just felt that he would have time "to get right with God." Just a few days later, as he hauled a load of logs, his truck left the road, hit an embankment, and the logs smashed into the cab. As I stood behind the casket to speak words of hope and comfort to a young widow, his sons, and parents, I was aware that his eternal salvation hinged upon a few brief seconds before death. Rejecting God! What a tragedy! What futility!

As we consider the brief record of Esau, we see a man rejecting God until he becomes rejected by God. Note the possibility, the incredulity, and the consequence of rejecting God.

I. *The possibility: man may reject God.*
   A. Because God has created man with the power of personal will.
      1. His grace must be desired.
      2. He seeks to reach man through man's will. He calls, "Come now and let us reason . . . " (Isaiah 1:18).
   B. Because God refuses to force His way into man's heart.
      1. He does not negate His self-imposed limitations.
      2. Christ is knocking, but we must open the door (e.g., Holman Hunt's picture, "Christ at the Door").
   C. In spite of God's love and desire that men accept Him.
      1. Predestination is always to life; never to death.
      2. But man may willfully reject God (Psalm 2:2 f.).
   D. Thus Esau could accept or reject God, but he rejected Him.
      1. He placed no value on spiritual things (25:32).
      2. He was completely a profane (secular) man (Hebrews 12:16).
      3. He married Canaanitish wives (26:34-35; 36:2).
         a. This was done to spite his father and mother.
         b. This was done contrary to the divine will.

II. *The incredulity: men reject God in spite of His effort to draw them to Himself* (Romans 2:4).
   A. In Esau's case, several factors encouraged his acceptance of God, but he rejected Him.
      1. A godly home. (It was far from perfect, but it was basically a spiritual home.)

a. Isaac was a loving, devoted father.
b. Abraham had provided a rich spiritual heritage.
c. The prayers of godly parents serve as a barrier to unlicensed sin (e.g., a young man at a drinking party thought: "What if my father walked in now?").
d. The great preacher, H. W. Beecher, said, "The memory of a godly mother kept me from many a sin."

2. A financially successful life (36:7).
   a. God means it for good. He bestows blessings on all.
   b. To many it becomes a curse (e.g., the rich young ruler).
3. A politically powerful influence.
   a. God means it for good.
   b. To some men it may be disastrous because they abuse it.

B. In man's case today, several factors encourage his acceptance of Christ, but man rejects Him.
   1. He can hardly help but hear someone point him to Christ.
      a. By way of television and radio.
      b. By the example of godly Christians.
   2. He has the Scriptures available.
   3. His rejection is incredible, and God declares, "Thou art inexcusable, O man" (Romans 2:1).

III. *The consequences: man cannot reject God without retribution.*
   A. Esau's personal influence for righteousness was nil. (Note the brevity of "the generations of Esau" 36:1-43. It plays out and he is dismissed from the divine record.)
   B. Esau faced the prospect of eternity without God.
   C. Esau's descendants opposed God.
   D. God's love becomes wrath when it is spurned. He is a "jealous God."

39

When Youth Dream Dreams

Genesis 37:5

It is a normal and necessary experience for youth to dream. Dreaming is a phenomenon common to all men. Extensive research has been done on the psychology of dreams. Dreams have been found usually to last no more than a few seconds, and a few minutes at the most, though we may feel that we have dreamed all night. Most dreams are also in "living color."

The Bible has quite a bit to say about dreams. It is one means of God's revelation to men. However, it is one of the lesser means of revelation. God revealed His will to Jacob at Bethel in a dream. Solomon was permitted one request by God in a dream, and he asked for wisdom. Gideon was assured of God's will through the dream of an enemy soldier. Daniel interpreted God's impending judgment on Babylon from Nebuchadnezzar's dream. God called Peter to preach to Cornelius and the Gentiles at Caesarea through a dream.

But the Bible also warns against overemphasizing the importance of a dream. False prophets depended upon dreams (Deuteronomy 13:2-5; Jeremiah 23:25). They were not to be heeded. In Ecclesiastes 5:3 we read, "a dream cometh through the multitude of business," that is, worry, or trouble. This very natural occurrence may be caused by mental or physical fatigue, or by a bad case of indigestion. But certain dreams are commendable.

In young Joseph's dreams we see that:

I. *Joseph occupied a special place in Jacob's family.*
  A. He was the young son of a favored wife, Rachel.
  B. He was pampered and petted by his father, Jacob (37:3).
    1. Jacob should have learned better from Isaac's favoritism toward Esau.
    2. Jacob gave Joseph a special coat: ankle-length and long-sleeved.
    3. Jacob excused Joseph from caring for sheep and made him an overseer.
    4. Jacob received the unfavorable report from Joseph concerning Joseph's brothers (37:2).
  C. He was hated by his brothers. (This was to be expected due to Joseph's talebearing and Jacob's favoritism.)

II. *God revealed His will for Joseph in two dreams.*
  A. The two dreams.
    1. The sheaves (37:7).

2. The sun, moon, and eleven stars (37:9).

B. The interpretation.

1. Joseph would be the recipient of the covenant blessings.

2. Joseph would be served by his brothers and parents some day. (Joseph probably should have kept these dreams private for personal edification).

C. The response.

1. The animosity of his brothers was expressed.

2. A rebuke from Jacob was declared, but he also reflected on them in his heart.

3. Their memory lingered with Joseph as a source of encouragement.

III. *Joseph's brothers sought to frustrate the will of God.*

A. They could not stand "this dreamer" (37:19).

B. They determined to dispose of him.

1. Reuben intervened to spare his life, but he compromised. His suggestion was not that of a loving brother (37:22).

2. Judah suggested that he be sold to a passing caravan (37:26 ff.).

a. In spite of Joseph's pleading with his brothers not to do this (42:21).

b. Without realizing that God was able to work out even this evil for His good.

c. Without being aware that God never abdicated His throne or forgot His promises.

IV. *Jacob experienced his greatest gain though he felt all was lost.*

A. He personally concluded that Joseph was dead (37:31-35).

1. He was deceived even as he had deceived others.

2. He found no comfort from family or friends.

B. He made the first reference to *Sheol,* life after death.

1. He thought Joseph was there.

2. Some day he knew that he would join him there.

V. *Joseph, the dreamer, was a slave in Potiphar's house* (37:36).

A. Because of his dreams, he was submissive to God.

B. Because of his dreams, he was uncompromising with evil.

C. Because of his dreams, he was committed to the will of God.

D. Because of his dreams, he found God's light in the midst of the darkness of unexplainable events.

1. When youth dream dreams, they should center on God's will.

2. When youth dream dreams, they should yield their lives to Him.

3. When youth dream dreams, they should begin to build the foundation on which they can erect the reality of their dreams.

4. When youth dream dreams, they should never let the presence of trying circumstances bring despair and defeat, but determine to persevere to the glory of God.

40

Can God Forgive Man's Worst Sin?

Genesis 38:26

Visit the Bourbon Streets of America. Observe sin in its most vile and arrogant expressions. Seemingly men tempt God to smite them with judgment. Multitudes are flocking to such places to sell their bodies to men and their souls to Satan. As Bob Harrington, the Chaplain of Bourbon Street, tells the owners of the bars and clubs in which he may preach, "If everyone of your employees are converted, you will have a complete new crew by tomorrow."

Listen with me as a welfare worker tells the hideous story of the plight of a retarded girl pregnant by her own father. Her older sisters told her to just be patient. She could soon leave home even as they had done. Of what worse sin could a man be guilty?

Join me as I talk to a man in prison. He is on trial for his life. The accusation is murder, taking the sacred life of another person in hatred and malice! Of what worse sin could a man be guilty?

Within the confines of Angola, the Louisiana State Penitentiary, on a quiet, sloping hill overlooking the Mississippi River is a little graveyard with very simple markings. At one time men were buried there without even the dignity of a suit of clothing. In one of those graves is the body of a young man whose parents would not even claim him. When the chaplain notified his mother of his death, she declared, "As far as I am concerned, I never had a son. Because of what he did I can never forgive him. Do as you wish with him."

There was a time when that could have been said by God about me. That could have been said about you. It could have been said about Judah who became a monument to the grace of God.

I. *Judah enjoyed a favored position.*
   A. He was born into the home of Jacob, God's chosen.
   B. He had repeated opportunities to trust God personally.
      1. He heard Jacob relate the events of Peniel where he wrestled with the Angel.
      2. He participated in Jacob's second Bethel experience.
   C. He failed to take advantage of his favored position.
      1. A parent's spiritual experience with God is not biologically transmitted.
      2. In colonial days, the state church of Massachusetts had Half-way Covenants.
      3. With God, however, there is no half-way salvation.

II. *Judah experienced the depths of depravity.* (Man either is moving upward, or downward. Judah was falling deeper into depravity).
   A. He married a Canaanite woman; he was not trusting in God (38:2).

1. He followed the foolish example of his Uncle Esau.
2. He saw the corrupt religious practices of the Canaanites revealing their moral and spiritual bankruptcy.
3. He had seen the vile treatment of his sister, Dinah, by the Shechemites.

B. Judah reared wicked, God-hating children; he was not serving God.
1. Er, his first son, was smitten by God (38:7).
2. Onan refused to fulfill the responsibility of a *goel* and was smitten.
a. A *goel* was a kinsman redeemer.
b. A *goel* was to redeem his brother's name; in this case Onan was to conceive a son in Er's name.
c. A *goel* was a type for Christ who always is faithful.

C. Judah failed to keep his word; he was not honest with Tamar (38:11, 14).

D. Judah was guilty of immorality; he committed adultery, or incest, with his daughter-in-law.

E. Judah was self-righteous and unjustly condemnatory; he proposed that Tamar be put to death (38:24c).

III. *Judah expressed his sin in confession* (38:26).
A. It was open, self-debasing, honest assessment of guilt.
B. It was an acceptance of others as even less vile than himself.
C. It was a recognition of the eternal consequences of sin (43:8 f.).
D. It was an acceptance of the One True God as the Superintendent of his life (44:15-16).

IV. *Judah was enshrined in Christ's lineage* (49:10; Matthew 1:3).
A. Men enshrine those who excel in a given area.
1. At Cooperstown, New York, is located the Baseball Hall of Fame.
2. At Anadarko, Oklahoma, famous Indians are recognized in the Indian Hall of Fame.

B. God enshrined Judah in the ancestry of Jesus Christ. God's grace won out!
1. Formerly he lived for self, but now he lived for others (44:33 f.).
2. Formerly he lived shamefully, but now he was sanctified.
3. Formerly he was filled with hate, but now he was filled with love.

C. You can be enshrined among the faithful in spite of your worst sins just as God did for Judah, if you will turn to Him in confession, repentance, and surrender.

41

Character That Endures

Genesis 39:1-23

Some people mistakenly confuse character with reputation, but they are different.

Reputation is what men think you are; character is what you really are.
Reputation is what you are in the exposure of the light; character is what you are in the secrecy of the night.
Reputation is subject to fluctuation depending upon men's evaluation; character is solid, stable, and constant regardless of men's estimation.
Reputation is effect; character is cause.

"Be not too concerned about reputation and success. Let them look out for themselves even though they should sometimes be under a cloud. Look well to character. It is the most cherished possession of life and any life that retains integrity of character is worth living" (R. L. Laurin, *Meet Yourself in the Bible*).

An agnostic had enrolled in a Baptist University. He resisted every effort to lead him to accept Christ. But, in front of him sat a very cultured, beautiful young sophomore with whom he often walked to the dormitory or to the drug store. One day he spoke of her captivating, special spirit that set her apart from others. She replied, "Oh, I did not know I had such a personality; but if I do, it is because of Christ. You see, I want to live like Him daily."

Even so, Joseph was a young man of character. His reputation often changed, but his character never did! Only one thing accounted for his commendable character—his allegiance to Yahweh God, the Lord God of his father (39:9). Above all else he sought to live each day in the light of God's will for his life.

Such dedication and consecration produced character that endured through all trying circumstances. It endured:

I. *In times of prosperity* (39:2).
  A. Joseph was confronted with the test of prosperity by becoming a supervisor over an unusually large amount of wealth. (This was unusual for a slave.)
    1. He manifested no bitterness over the circumstances that wrested him from his father's house.
    2. He expressed a perfect and peaceful surrender to God.
    3. He realized that God providentially controlled his life.
      a. Wycliff translated "prosperous" as "a luckie fellowe." His position was not luck, but divine providence.

b. He illustrated the truth of the proverb, "A poor man can be happy; but a happy man can't be poor."

B. Some people cannot endure the test of prosperity.
  1. A little wealth often makes one feel independent! But we are never so.
  2. Today we live in an affluent society.
    a. When a certain family in my hometown of Saint Francisville, Louisiana, were poor, they were faithful church attenders. But when they had a little money, the theater took precedence over God's house.
    b. We possess so much more today than a generation ago.
    c. There are so many more attractions calling for one's attention.
  3. In our busy schedules so little time is left for God.
    a. A minister on the Mississippi Gulf Coast said, "There is no need to visit a home with a boat in the yard."
    b. A mission pastor, who moved into a model community near Baltimore, Maryland, asserted that most of the people living in that community felt no real need for God.

C. God can mightily use those who remain true through prosperity as He used Joseph.

II. *In times of inflamed passions* (39:9, 12).

A. Joseph repeatedly faced the temptation of immorality.
  1. Not just once, but again and again Potiphar's wife tried to seduce Joseph.
  2. Finally, Joseph had to fight from her clutches and flee. (There was smoke, but no fire!)
    a. Sin is not in the temptation, but in our yielding to it.
    b. "It is better to lose a good coat than a good conscience" (Matthew Henry, *Commentary on the Whole Bible).*
  3. Joseph's refusal was based on two grounds.
    a. His allegiance to the trust Potiphar placed in him.
    b. His allegiance to God in whom he placed his trust.
    c. He realized that the two cannot be separated.

B. We are confronted daily by the temptations of a sex-saturated society.
  1. C. H. Henry wrote in *Christianity Today,* "Americans have sex thrust upon them every waking hour of their day."
  2. Malcolm Muggeridge said in *Esquire,* "America is the most sex-ridden country in the history of the world."
  3. A Christian attitude toward sexuality and an adherence to God's standard is essential today in our daily lives.

C. We should be careful not to endanger ourselves by fanning the flames of passions.
  1. Many things today are designed to arouse passions.
    a. Movies.
    b. Books.

c. Dancing
d. Drinking.
e. Petting.

2. The Christian should abstain from the appearance of evil.

III. *In times of imprisonment* (39:20-21).

A. Unjust imprisonment could bring disappointment and disillusionment.

B. Such imprisonment could cause self-pity and a tendency to blame God.

1. Job's wife did so in similar circumstances.
2. Joseph did not, but instead he blessed God.

C. Similar imprisonments may develop patience and responsiveness.

1. Joyce Carmichel said, "We never know what God may have in mind for us."
2. Some of our prisoners of war in Vietnam were drawn closer to God in prison.
3. Joseph waited, and God ultimately rewarded him. His character endured.

Conclusion:

Christian character begins at the cross of Christ, and develops through faithful, daily commitment to Him in spite of daily circumstances.

42

Lessons Learned in Prison

Genesis 40

If the story of Joseph's life ended with this chapter, the imprisonment of Joseph would have been a gross miscarriage of justice and a blemish on the holy character of God. It is not the end, however, but a means by which Joseph stepped from prison to the premiership of ancient Egypt. Furthermore, it was a means used by God to preserve His chosen people.

Harold Dye in *The Weaver* told of watching a Navaho woman weaving a blanket. She patiently and purposefully wove various colors of yarn into the blanket to produce her desired pattern. He then wrote that God so weaves various strands into our lives. Often this includes suffering, disappointment, and discouragement, but ultimately it produces God's chosen pattern.

Imprisonment teaches a man many lessons, some good and some bad. Seldom have I met a man in jail or in the penitentiary who deserved to be there, if we accept his story. But, usually it is the last resort to teach them certain lessons. God was teaching Joseph certain lessons that would constantly bless his life and also his people.

He learned:

I. *Patience in the midst of distress.*
  A. Joseph developed patience through trying circumstances.
    1. In spite of being sold into slavery by his brothers.
    2. In spite of being unjustly accused of immorality.
    3. In spite of being unjustly imprisoned for years.
      a. Preparing him for future days when he would be misunderstood as chief tax collector.
      b. Preparing him for the seven-year cycles which doubtless produced impatience in others.
      c. Preparing him for a most demanding office which God used to preserve Jacob's family.
  B. We need to learn patience in the testing times of life (Luke 21:19; James 1:3-4).
    1. We are creatures of impatience. We want our desires satisfied *now!*
    2. We at times pray as the man who prayed, "Lord, give me patience, and I mean right now."
    3. Henry Ward Beecher spoke of a businessman who faced bankruptcy, but he stayed on top through constant effort. He was advised to "let patience have her perfect work." His reply

was, "If you faced what I did, you would know patience." Yet, patience is just what he needed.

II. *Piety in the face of disappointment.*
   A. Joseph dreamed dreams of glory and grandeur.
      1. In spite of the constant presence of danger.
      2. In spite of his false accusation by others.
      3. In spite of his imprisonment.
      4. In spite of the fact that such dreams appeared to be mere illusions.
   B. Joseph determined to live each day for God.
      1. He earned the respect of his jailer (40:4).
      2. He won acceptance by the chief butler and baker (40:8).
         a. He told them of his God.
         b. He quietly demonstrated his piety daily before them.
         c. His piety was seen in his life as a "living sacrifice."
   C. As Joseph we are to determine to live each day for God regardless of the apparent return.
      1. To serve God for what He may give us is to "buy" God.
      2. To be faithful to God in every situation is to please God (Job 1:21).

III. *Purpose in the course of discipline* (40:14-15).
   A. Joseph was aware that "God ruleth in the affairs of men."
   B. Joseph sensed an ultimate purpose in his discipline.
      1. God was preparing him for a position of international importance.
         a. The dignity and self-control which were expressed later before Pharaoh were being developed in prison.
         b. The interpretation of the dreams of the butler and the baker prepared him for even larger service to Pharaoh.
      2. God is often revealing His divine purpose for us through hardship in our lives.
         a. It was so for Daniel in a den of lions.
         b. It was true for Paul in a Roman prison.
         c. It was true for John on Patmos; for John Bunyan in Bedford's prison; for George Fox, the Quaker, in Lancaster Castle; for Adoniram Judson in a Burmese cell; for Bill Wallace in a Chinese torture chamber; and for Herbert Caudill and David Fite in a Castro Cuban confine.

IV. *Perseverance in spite of discouragement* (40:14, 21, 23).
   A. Joseph had many reasons to become discouraged and quit, but he never gave up.
      1. He lost his favored position in Jacob's family.
      2. He forfeited his trusted position in Potiphar's house.
      3. He languished forgotten in prison for two years after the butler's promised intervention.
   B. We also often face discouraging experiences in life and want to quit, but we must not quit.

1. It may be a trying session with a Sunday school class.
2. It may be a committee or a deacon's meeting that did not accomplish just what we thought it should.
3. It may be when we falter or fall back into sin.
4. It may be when someone whom we have trusted disappoints us.
5. It may be when incident after incident brings more and more backsets.
6. It may be as when a mother asked me concerning her efforts to reach a wayward son, "But where can I quit?"

V. *Peace in the experience of apparent defeat.*

A. Joseph suffered vicariously as a type of Christ.

1. In the beginning the prison experience seemed to spell out defeat.
2. Through the experience Joseph possessed an inner peace.
3. In the end defeat was turned to victory.

B. We are called upon to bear our cross for Christ.

1. To some persons this may seem to be a defeat.
2. But in the experience we come to know peace in the presence of Christ who declared, "I am with you alway."
3. And in the end we are assured of victory.

43

From Prison to Premiership

Genesis 41:14-43, 46-48, 53-54, 57

In Joseph's life is found a true story of "from rags to riches." Only one in whom truly "the Spirit of God is" could be taken from the depths of prison to the pinnacle of power in ancient Egypt.

Joseph entered the scene of Egyptian history at a time when nationality or race would mean very little to the reigning monarch. This occurred during the Hyksos Period. The Hyksos were invaders from upper Asia Minor and Russia mixed with Indo-Europeans who had invaded Egypt and gained ascendancy. In recent times the Egyptian ruler would choke with rage if an Israeli held such a position as Joseph did. But it was not so in Joseph's day. He was God's man for trying times.

In this chapter we see:

I. *The adversity of Joseph.*

(Character is never developed in a crisis; it is merely expressed.)

A. He enjoyed relative ease during his early years in Canaan.

B. He felt the devastating blows of adversity for the next thirteen years.

1. He was betrayed by his brothers.
2. He was enslaved by his brothers to the Ishmaelites and then to the Egyptians.
3. He was imprisoned through the false accusations of Potiphar's wife.
4. He was forgotten in prison by those whom he had befriended.

C. He learned many necessary lessons during this adverse period. (Adversity is an excellent teacher.)

1. He learned patience in the face of distressing circumstances.
2. He learned dependence upon God: "My grace is sufficient."
3. He learned to be concerned for his fellowman.
4. He learned perseverance and dependability as he faced responsibility.

II. *The anxiety of Pharaoh* (41:8).

A. He was disturbed by two dreams.

1. The first dream was of seven fat cows and seven lean cows that came up out of the Nile.
2. The second dream was of seven full ears of corn which were consumed by seven thin ears of corn that followed.

B. He expressed his anxiety.

1. He called for those who practiced sorcery.

a. The Bible expressly forbids this practice.

b. It is dealing with evil powers and is satanic.
2. He called on his astrologers and his wise men.
3. He finally heard of Joseph and sent for him.
4. He was willing to try anything that remotely promised an answer.

C. He lacked a stabilizing dependence on God (cf. Matthew 6:34).

III. *The answer of God* (41:15-16).

A. God is concerned with the affairs of the nations of His world.
B. God had given the dreams regarding the future.
C. God had placed Joseph there for this occasion.
1. Joseph witnessed of God as The One True God (41:25, 28, 32). (He used the unusual occurrence of the definite article with God.)
2. Joseph provided the interpretation of the dreams.
D. God revealed that they were to prepare for an extended famine.
1. Pharaoh was directed to select the right man, Joseph (41:33).
2. Joseph proposed that he impose a 20 percent tax on all crops and preserve it.
E. God's eternal answer for the needs of man is to bring life through Jesus Christ.

IV. *The appointment of a premier* (41:39-40).

A. Pharaoh exalted Joseph to a position of authority.
1. This was far beyond Joseph's expectation.
2. This was the beginning of the fulfillment of his dreams.
B. Pharaoh elevated Joseph next to himself; he became second in command.
1. The ring: signified his royal authority.
2. The linen: symbolized his sacred standing and dignity.
3. The gold chain: portrayed his wealth.
4. The chariot: depicted his position of honor. (Chariots were introduced to Egypt by the Hyksos.)

V. *The advancement of God's kingdom* (41:57).

A. Joseph's appointment was for Joseph's good.
B. Joseph's appointment was for Egypt's good.
C. Joseph's appointment was also for Israel's good. Israel and Egypt became mutually aligned. (They shall also be so aligned in the future worship of God, cf. Isaiah 19:23-25.)
D. Joseph's appointment helped to advance God's kingdom.
1. The experience of Joseph illustrates what God can do through one man who is yielded to Him.
2. The experience of Joseph may be reflected in the conversion of a person who yields to God today.

Conclusion:
God can still take the littleness of our lives and exalt them in His own greatness. We may not become premiers, as Joseph did, but we can become sons of God and children of the King.

44

The Persistence of a Guilty Conscience

Genesis 42:1-24, 35-38

Key Verse: 42:22

One day a man walked into a police station in Houston, Texas, and said to a surprised police sergeant, "I am the man you are looking for. I escaped from the state penitentiary twenty-five years ago." He was a successful, prosperous, middle-aged businessman with a family. When asked why he gave himself up, he replied, "I could not live with my conscience."

An apparently successful young man was a vice-president of a bank in Louisiana. One day two Treasury agents of the federal government approached him and said, "You are under arrest." He replied, "Thank God, I don't know how much longer I could have borne it." In just over two years he had embezzled nearly forty thousand dollars, but he could not quiet his conscience.

A man sat in my study and sobbed out a story of past unfaithfulness to his wife and family. He said, "I must tell her. I can't stand it any longer." Again, conscience could not be subdued and silenced.

This was also a problem to Joseph's brothers. In this chapter, we note:

I. *The presence of human conscience.*

A. God has provided man with a conscience, or moral awareness.

1. The word *conscience* means literally "to know with."
2. It implies "to know with God."

B. Man forfeited his claim to an innocent conscience by sin.

C. Man's conscience may be in one of several states.

1. A regretting conscience. One may truly regret the deed, but continue to be involved in specific wrongdoing.
2. A remembering conscience. A person may be keenly aware of his past wrongs and yet be unable to experience a sense of forgiveness.
3. A rebelling conscience.
   a. May become hardened and seared (e.g., a man had committed a brutal murder and was apprehended. His only regret was that he was caught).
   b. Is certainly not to be trusted. If such a conscience is your guide it will lead you astray.
4. A restored conscience. This is man's need and should be his goal.

II. *The pleasure of a clear conscience.*

A. Was experienced by Joseph due to his fear of God (42:18).

1. In regard to his brothers. He was testing them to see what the past twenty-one years had done for them.

a. Joseph faced the temptation of revenge. (They had not forgotten what they had done to him, 42:13).
b. His awareness of God's providence delivered him from seeking vengeance.
2. In regard to Potiphar and his wife.
a. Joseph faced the temptation of lust.
b. His commitment to God kept him pure (39:9).
3. In regard to Pharaoh.
a. Joseph faced the temptation of ambition.
b. His faith in God led him to give God the glory. "It is The One True God that reveals dreams" (41:16).
B. May be experienced by men today as they fear God and serve Him.
1. It is a source of joy in daily life.
2. It is a source of peace each day.

III. *The persistence of a guilty conscience.*
A. Was experienced by Joseph's brothers due to their unconfessed sin.
1. They were ill at ease at the very mention of Egypt (42:1). (They probably jumped every time they heard it mentioned.)
a. They did not want to talk about Egypt, or Joseph, or a coat, or a goat's blood.
b. They did not want to go to Egypt.
c. They did not want to be reminded of Egypt. (They were just as a guilty sinner who is willing to talk about anything except his sin.)
2. They vividly remembered the pleading of Joseph (42:21).
3. They came to admit their guilt before God (42:21-22).
B. May be experienced by those who reject the Lord and rebel against Him.
1. Man must cope repeatedly with a sense of guilt.
a. As Bob Harrington said, "I felt so guilty that when the school principal would clear his voice over the public address system I headed for the office."
b. Many times we feel so uneasy even when our parents call us (e.g., one night my mother threatened to call some parents about the conduct of my friends. I begged her not to do it, because I was just as guilty).
2. Man's greatest guilt—crucifying the Lord Jesus Christ—is shared by us all (Romans 3:23).

IV. *The cure of a guilty conscience.*
A. Take it to God in confession (I John 1:9).
B. Turn from the sin. Close the door on it.
C. Make restitution to those who have been hurt by your actions.
D. By faith accept the pardon that Christ provides through His blood.

Conclusion:

A young woman was in the psychiatric ward of a great hospital. She asked me to counsel with her, and told of terrible guilt for wrong deeds committed fourteen years previously. In prayer she confessed it to God and was forgiven, learned to accept herself, and came to enjoy a *restored conscience*. This is the only way to forgiveness and joy.

45

The Eternal Consequences of Sin

Genesis 43:1-10, 13-17, 26-34

Key Verses: 43:8-9

A man's spiritual maturity can usually be determined by his sensitivity to sin. A light view of sin and a mild reaction to its ultimate consequences usually betray a flippant, irreverent, meaningless relationship to God.

Judah, however, had undergone a great transition in his attitude toward sin. As a result, he won the trust of his father along with the approval of God.

Judah's attitude toward sin was that:

I. *Sin is real, and universal.*
   A. Expressing itself in rebellion toward God and in rejection of one's fellowman.
      1. E.g., Cain, who slew Abel, his brother.
      2. E.g., David, who was guilty of adultery with Bathsheba.
      3. E.g., Demas, who forsook Paul. (He chose the world for himself rather than serving people for Christ's sake.)
   B. Exemplifying itself in the unbrotherly conduct of Judah and his brothers.
      1. The brothers could not undo what they had done to Joseph.
      2. Judah could not erase his sin with his daughter-in-law.
      3. Even their father was not without guilt (43:6).
         a. He was not trusting God completely.
         b. He was suggesting that they did not have to tell the full truth.
   C. Ensnaring even God's chosen leaders in its power.
      1. Adam was innocent in Paradise, but he fell. (So the answer to sin is not slum clearance.)
      2. Noah was a "perfect" man, but he fell into drunkenness.
      3. Abraham was the Father of the Righteous and the Friend of God, but he fell into dishonesty regarding Sarai.
      4. Simon Peter was one of the chosen twelve, but he fell into denials and swearing.
   D. Encompassing each of us in its sway.
      1. It may be difficult and painful to admit.
      2. It must be confessed individually, nevertheless.

II. *Sin incurs penalty and demands payment.*
   A. In admitting a personal indebtedness.
      1. The brothers were aware of a debt and the peril of not meeting its payment.

2. Their consciences were convicted.
   a. Of their sin against Joseph.
   b. Of finding money in their sacks after their first trip (43:19-22).
3. They sought to effect payment for their wrongs with "double money," but they had the wrong "currency."

B. In presenting oneself as a personal sacrifice.
   1. Judah offered himself as "surety", i.e., a guarantee.
   2. He refused to suggest that his children could be called to suffer the consequences of his wrongs, as Reuben had done.
   3. He offered to bear the consequences personally.

C. In realizing that the ultimate penalty is death.
   1. "The wages of sin" is eternal death (Romans 6:23).
   2. "There is a way that seemeth right to man, but the end thereof are the ways of death" (Proverbs 16:25).
   3. God warns of and requires the penalty for sin.

III. *Sin incurs personal guilt, and is eternal in its consequences.*

A. Judah realized that he could never escape sin's eternal consequences (43:9).
   1. Many feel that they can "get by."
      a. One may get by men, but not God.
      b. One may get by for a while, but not forever.
   2. Men should acknowledge that sin brings "blame," or guilt.

B. Joseph returned good for evil by putting his brothers to the test.
   1. He saw God's earlier promises to him being fulfilled.
   2. He arranged them in order by ages (43:33). (This must have aroused their anxiety.)
   3. He gave Benjamin five times as much as any other brother.
      a. The brothers manifested no sign of jealousy.
      b. Judah was doubtless cognizant of his responsibility.
   4. He viewed them as guilty of rejecting him although they were unaware of their predicament.
      a. They all, except Benjamin, shared the guilt.
      b. They had no adequate means of making atonement.

C. We stand guilty before God of rejecting Him.
   1. Sin brings eternal consequences.
   2. But Jesus is the eternal sacrifice for sin.
   3. He desires and is able to remove it eternally if we will yield ourselves to Him.

46

You Cannot Go Home Without Your Brother

Genesis 44:1-34

Key Verses: 44:30-34

Through discipline and trial Joseph was testing his brothers. He had trusted them once, and they had sold him into slavery. In sincerity he had forgiven them; but could they be trusted again? Were their lives the same, or had they experienced a change through the ensuing years?

I. *The problem: An erring brother* (44:1-14).

A. Apprehended along the way for stealing a special cup.

1. The "divining" cup had been planted in a certain sack. The word *divining* is related to the word *serpent (nahash),* and was a pagan symbol of spiritual power.

a. Some people today claim such powers of sorcery.

b. Other persons experiment with different forms of sorcery or magic. (A well-known figure believed that he had communicated with his son who had committed suicide. This twice-divorced man attained great ecclesiastical rank, but he lacked personal, spiritual maturity. He was always searching, but never finding.)

2. The divining cup was found in Benjamin's sack following a methodical search.

3. The presence of the divining cup incriminated Benjamin as being guilty of theft and ingratitude.

B. Appeared before the prime minister, Joseph, for judgment regarding his crime.

1. They had proposed that the guilty one would die and the others would be slaves.

2. Joseph decreed that only the guilty party should be punished.

3. They could have left Benjamin and gone free, but they all returned to face judgment together.

II. *The solution: a substitutionary sacrifice.*

A. Joseph claimed "divine" power (44:15).

1. Previously Joseph had rejected this power, knowing that it belongs to God.

2. This assertion was designed for its effect upon the brothers.

B. Judah asserted his faith in the One True God (44:16).

1. He willingly faced danger by rebuking one whom he thought to be a pagan sovereign.

2. He acknowledged God's providential working in their lives by declaring that they were receiving just retribution for their sins.

3. He admitted that sin's debt must be paid by refusing to excuse it.

C. Judah offered to be the substitute for his brother (44:33).

1. Judah, the ancestor of Jesus, was a type of Christ. (J. R. Sampey said, "This is the most beautiful and noble piece of moving literature.")

2. Judah would willingly take his brother's place, just as Christ did for us.

a. E.g., a Confederate soldier secured a replacement for himself and went back to his family. The replacement died at Gettysburg. From then on he lived for the man who died in his stead.

b. E.g., at Harrodsburg, Kentucky, I stood one day on a slave auction block. I remembered that I had been enslaved, but Jesus redeemed me with His precious blood. I must live for Him.

III. *The deduction: a personal responsibility.*

A. You cannot go back home.

1. I enjoyed my early years in Orange, Texas, living in the house of a Swedish couple named Jorgenson. They had a gallery and a small yard. Years later I tried to return, but found that the house had been removed to make room for an office building. You cannot go back "home."

2. I went to my grandfather's old home places at Belle Isle and Cheniere Tigre, Louisiana. The once-thriving community is now gone and covered with marsh grass and twisted oaks. Eighty-seven-year-old Uncle Granvell Lee pointed out the spots where the house, barn, fields of cotton and corn had been, but now they are part of the marsh. As we left, he whispered, "Bye-bye old place. I don't guess I'll see you again." He had been away for fifty years. You cannot go back "home."

3. On our honeymoon we stayed in a beautiful, tree-surrounded, rustic motel cottage. We had difficulty finding a place, but the owners had provided us a cabin and treated us royally. Several years later we returned for an overnight visit. We stopped, looked at its dilapidated condition, and drove on. You cannot go back "home."

4. You cannot go back home in many respects.

a. To past opportunities.

b. To sins committed in the past.

c. To decisions of importance.

B. You cannot go home *without your brother*.

1. You are your brother's keeper. You cannot go without him.

2. As Christ gave Himself for you, you are to give yourself to others.

3. As Judah did, give yourself to others, and to Christ.

4. Determine to take your brother with you.

47

Is the Lad with You?

Genesis 44:18-34

What is a boy? Someone has said that he is a bundle of energy with chocolate on his nose. Someone else has said that he is perpetual motion with a frog, a string, and an apple core in his pocket. But one thing about it, boys are with us. What would this world be without boys? Sometimes we wonder what in the world we will do with them; but what would we do without them?

Joseph had been sold into Egyptian slavery. Jacob's other sons had heartlessly led their father to believe that Joseph had been killed by a wild animal. Jacob's love was then transferred to Benjamin.

On the first trip to Egypt, Premier Joseph demanded that Simeon remain as hostage while the others returned to bring their youngest brother, Benjamin. Jacob refused to permit this. Reuben offered his children as surety, but Jacob refused. Later Judah made a similar request, but he pledged himself as surety (43:9). Jacob acquiesced. Judah realized that when they returned home Jacob would ask, "Is the lad with you?"

I. *Every boy needs a man.*
   A. A man should be aware of his influence (e.g., "Every man is some boy's hero").
      1. You are probably a hero to some boy of whom you may not be aware.
      2. As a teen-ager I had a bitter disappointment when I saw a man whom I admired for his moral principles drinking a can of beer.
   B. A boy normally looks to a man as a hero.
      1. He wants to be identified with a man.
      2. He may have to take big steps, or walk "double time," but he wants to have male company.
      3. On a daily national television program the host spoke to a young tennis star of the great influence that a woman had had on him. He retorted, "It wasn't a woman, but a man."

II. *Every man needs a boy.* (It does not necessarily have to be one's own child.)
   A. A man needs the challenge of a boy (e.g., "A man stands no taller than when he stoops to help a boy").
      1. A man needs the idealism of a boy.
      2. A man needs a challenge to be something above the ordinary.
   B. A man needs to realize a boy's expectation of him.
      1. One man was moved deeply when his son prayed, "Lord, help me to be like my daddy."

2. In a Washington, D.C., restaurant, a lad ordered "whatever my daddy takes." His father, who usually took whiskey, ordered a lemonade.

III. *Christian men must accept the challenge for Christian leadership.*

A. We must realize that the young men whom we influence today will determine the kind of church we have in fifteen years.

1. A German school teacher bowed to his students when he entered the room. When he was asked why, he said, "Because a genius may be there." From that room came Martin Luther.
2. One day at Esther, Louisiana, I saw a giant tree. My grandfather had planted it as a sprout. Then it grew.
3. So what we plant today will grow to bless the future.

B. We must recognize the moral consequences of failure (43:9).

Conclusion:
So the question is still important, "Is the lad with you?"

48

Gratitude That Prompts True Worship

Genesis 46:1-7

Jacob was no stranger to the site of Beersheba. At Beersheba Jacob's grandfather Abraham worshiped Yahweh, and God revealed to Abraham the truth that He is the God of eternity (21:33). At Beersheba Abraham lived after offering his son Isaac to God (22:19). Following a difficulty with the Philistines over wells and water rights, Jacob's father, Isaac, lived at Beersheba and there worshiped God (26:23-25). At Beersheba Jacob lived as a youth with his parents, Isaac and Rebekah (26:32-34, by inference).

"A lot of water had passed under the bridge" since those days. Jacob had spent nearly twenty years in Haran. He returned to Canaan as the bearer of the covenant promises of God. His family had grown and become prosperous. Joseph had been thought dead, but then, in the midst of a serious famine, he was found to be in Egypt. He had sent for his father and the entire family. With rejoicing Israel had begun his journey to Egypt. The journey took him past Beersheba. What fond memories and recollections of boyhood days raced through his thoughts. What reverent memories of moments spent with God flooded his mind, and he turned aside to worship!

In this experience, we see:

I. *The need for true worship.*
  A. Because man is a worshiping creature.
    1. He is created "in his image" with a capacity for God.
    2. He possesses a God-shaped emptiness that only God can fill.
  B. Because of the abundance of false worship (Romans 1:20-25).
    1. The idolator is evidence of false worship (cf. Isaiah 44:9-20).
    2. Man's deeply religious nature has been prostituted in many expressions.
      a. America has experienced a rise of false cults: non-Christian, sub-Christian, and anti-Christian.
        (1) Mary Baker Eddy founded Christian Science.
        (2) Charles Russell gave birth to Jehovah's Witnesses.
        (3) Joseph Smith became the founder of Mormonism.
        (4) Anton La Vey began the Church of Satan movement.
        (5) Hari Krishna advocates are found in our cities.
        (6) Oriental religions are gaining in popularity.
      b. Russia, though atheistic, has fostered a religion of the state. (Grey Allison told of a Russian guide who said, "Lenin is our god.")
      c. China has made a god of Mao Tse-tung)

C. Because Jesus Christ has provided the way for true worship (John 4:23 f.).
D. Because it provides maximum development for man's soul.
   1. The body needs the nourishment of physical food.
   2. The soul needs the nourishment of worship, which is spiritual food.
   3. The person who should find himself in heaven but cannot enjoy the experience of worship on earth is to be pitied.
   4. A person is strengthened and enriched by expressing his gratitude in true worship. (A young man had a habit of slipping into his church building each day at noon for a few moments. His pastor asked him one day, "Jim, what are you doing?" He said, "Well, pastor, one day Jesus came to me and said, 'Jim, it's Jesus.' I took Him as my Savior. Now I come to say to Him each day on my brief noon hour, 'Jesus, it's Jim.' And I go on to serve Him.")

II. *The results of true worship* (46:2-4).
A. An awareness of the presence of God.
   1. To live each day knowing that Christ is ever-present is a joy. (A reporter wrote of a young soldier's conversation at Con Thien, Vietnam, saying, "It always came around to God." Psalm 91 is a note of welcome comfort in such a surrounding.)
   2. In our everyday activities we need this awareness of God. (This awareness is illustrated by a little boy who was throwing a ball up in the air and catching it. He was "playing catch with God").
B. An acceptance of the purpose of God (46:5).
   1. Jacob had serious reservations about going to Egypt.
      a. God was using a desperate situation—a famine—to secure obedience.
      b. What Israel wanted done in Palestine—building a mighty nation—God could do best in Egypt.
   2. Jacob's remaining reservations were removed in worship.
      a. God's purpose is best seen in true worship.
      b. God's purpose is always for our ultimate good. (I was called to preach over a long period. I weighed it carefully and critically while I was alone. At that time I refused. But, while I was involved in corporate worship, I responded affirmatively. This road has, at times, been difficult; but if I had many lives, and had to make the decision again, I would want to use every one of them in preaching and teaching His Word.)
C. An acceptance of the provisions of God.
   1. Jacob preferred to have his needs met in Canaan so that he could remain there.
   2. Jacob perceived that God chose to meet his needs in Egypt as

he engaged in worship. (His fear became faith.)

3. Jacob was convinced that God would provide (22:14). (This needs to be our motto.)
   a. To meet our physical and spiritual needs. (When my father surrendered to the ministry in 1939, some people thought him to be crazy. With a growing family, he enrolled in high school at Acadia Baptist Academy in Louisiana. We may have become tired of beans and rice, but we never went hungry. God provided for our needs.)
   b. To provoke gratitude for the present and assurance concerning the future.

D. An acknowledgment of the power of God (46:3). *El,* God, means "strength."
1. Jacob knew that the God of power and might would superintend his way.
2. So Jacob led them, seventy-five persons in all, into Egypt where God made them the great nation that He desired.
   a. God, who could overthrow Sodom, throw down the walls of Jericho, and care for Jacob, can provide safety and security for us.
   b. Gratitude for such protection should prompt us to worship.

49

When Israel Blessed Egypt

Key Verse: Genesis 47:1-31

In light of ancient and modern history the idea of Israel blessing Egypt is difficult to imagine. Since the founding of the modern nation of Israel in 1947, hatred and conflict have seethed between these nations of the Mideast. In light of such animosity, this chapter reads as a strange record of their relationship.

Today a small part of the Egyptian population is Jewish, but their position is not an enviable one. This situation did not always exist, though it has been true in nearly every period in the history of Egyptian-Israeli relations.

According to Genesis 47, God overruled the natural animosity and prejudice between these peoples to bring Israel and Egypt together for Israel's good. According to historians the Hyksos rulers were also foreigners in Egypt and thus favorable toward Israel. Thus in wisdom and might God truly worked all things for good to those who loved Him and were called according to His purpose. In turn, Israel was a blessing to Egypt:

I. *By a profitable migration to Egypt* (47:1-12).
  A. It was divinely inspired.
    1. Joseph had been sent earlier to make preparation.
    2. Jacob's reluctance to go to Egypt had been overcome.
      a. By the message sent from Joseph.
      b. By the worship experience at Beersheba in which God revealed His purpose for Israel.
  B. It was humanly difficult.
    1. To leave the land of promise, never to see it again.
    2. To forsake the burial place of loved ones.
    3. To move from one's land without any plans to return.
      a. This feeling was expressed by a returning soldier who tipped his hat to the Statue of Liberty and said, "If you ever see me again, you will have to turn around."
      b. When I first saw that colossal statue, I thought of Emma Lazarus's words that are engraved on the pedestal:

> Give me your tired, your poor,
> Your huddled masses yearning to breathe free,
> The wretched refuse of your teeming shore.
> Send these, the homeless, tempest-tossed to me.
> I lift my lamp beside the golden door!

I then thought of the many heartaches and tears shed by

millions of persons as they left their country to seek a new way of life. It is never an easy decision to do so.

C. It was significantly blessed.
   1. Prejudice against shepherds was divinely used to isolate the Hebrews in Goshen.
      a. Egyptians held shepherds in contempt. Their artists depicted shepherds as lame, crippled, and dirty.
      b. Jobs were open to them caring for the royal herds.
   2. The choice land of the delta was provided for them.
   3. Food was provided through Pharaoh's graciousness.

II. *By a wise administration over Egypt* (47:13-26).
   A. In implementing economy measures during the years of plenty.
   B. In instilling hope during the long years of famine. (An archaeological discovery revealed a time when the Nile failed to rise for seven years. It was dated about 1700 B.C.)
      1. In our own country a depression began about 1929. Millionaires became paupers. Thousands of people committed suicide.
      2. In Egypt the people turned to Pharaoh who sent them to Joseph.
   C. In administering a wise and equitable program.
      1. During its initial phase he sold grain for money.
      2. During the second phase he traded grain for cattle and livestock.
      3. During the subsequent phase he bartered grain for their lands.
      4. Following the acquisition of their lands by the state, Joseph provided the people grain for seed in return for one-fifth of the harvest. (This was a small assessment when compared to some of the ancient parallels.)
   D. In maintaining a successful program that assured relief and self-respect.

III. *By a victorious separation from Egypt* (47:27-31).
   A. Because Israel's eye was not on the fortunes of Egypt.
      1. He did not desire its wealth.
      2. He was but a pilgrim there.
      3. He wanted to be buried with Abraham and Isaac.
   B. Because Israel had no fear of approaching death.
   C. Because Israel's real desire was for God.
      1. He worshiped Him (47:31).
      2. He was in Egypt, but Egypt was not in him.
      3. Thus his life, family, and example was a blessing to Egypt.

50

The Redeemer of Israel

Genesis 48:9-19

We have a glorious promise in Philippians 1:6 that "he which hath begun a good work in you will perfect it until the day of Jesus Christ." That is, God through His Son Jesus Christ works in the heart and life of each Christian to develop the Christian into that which God wants him to be. By chastening, challenging, convicting, and molding, Christ perfects His followers.

Israel experienced this in his own life. He was aware that the Angel had worked in his life for many years. Yet, he had nothing of which he could boast except in the redeeming work of the Angel who later manifested Himself in the person of Christ.

I. *Redeemed him from the littleness of self.*
  A. Setting Jacob free from his undue concern for self. (He had not been concerned for Esau or for others. In this he had been encouraged by Rebekah.)
    1. In obtaining the birthright from Esau.
    2. In deceiving Isaac to receive the blessing.
  B. Setting Jacob free from self to fellowship with God.
    1. Selfish ambition is a deification of self.
    2. Self-righteousness and self-achievement stand as a barrier separating man from God.
    3. A meaningful admission that we are sinners may be difficult, but we can do nothing alone to redeem ourselves.
    4. Paul is an example of letting "self" keep one from God.
      a. He was zealous for his own righteousness.
      b. He was ambitious for his personal exaltation.
      c. He was redeemed by Christ when he met Him. From then on, Christ was everything and he was nothing.

II. *Redeemed him from the tyranny of material things.*
  A. From being interested in driving a hard bargain. (He became known as "the Deceiver.")
    1. With Esau and his birthright. He took advantage of his brother's needs. (Some may say, "Well, that is business." But it is still sin to unfairly capitalize on another person's difficulties.)
    2. With Laban for wages. He used ringstreaked rods at the watering troughs hoping to secure an added advantage.
    3. With Esau at his return. He first thought that he could buy Esau's favor when he returned.

B. Through losing his beloved Rachel, which opened his eyes to really important values.
C. Through experiencing the odious events surrounding the sins of Dinah and her brothers, which made him realize the folly of pursuing material things.
D. Through living during days of famine, which caused treasures to tarnish and led him to turn his eyes on his Shepherd.
E. Through a growing awareness that material values are not lasting.
   1. Paul warned, "The love of money is the root of all evil" (I Timothy 6:10).
   2. It is no sin to be successful, but this is not to be our primary goal.

III. *Redeemed him from his fear of Esau.*
   A. Leading him to return, though fearfully, to the Promised Land.
      1. He tried bribery by sending lavish gifts at intervals.
      2. He tried cunning by separating his family into two groups.
      3. He trusted self until he was crippled.
      4. Then he trusted God because of his Peniel experience when he wrestled with the Angel who blessed him.
   B. Leading him to discover that God was adequate to protect him.
      1. By changing Esau's heart after he had vowed to kill Jacob.
      2. By teaching Jacob that God would bless His children as they depended upon Him.
      3. By turning a dreaded meeting into a glorious family reunion.
   C. Leading him to live confidently, though cautiously, in the land.
      1. Christ advised that we be wise as serpents but harmless as doves. Thus we must watch our enemies.
      2. Basically we must confidently trust the Lord and diligently exercise caution in our daily lives.

IV. *Redeemed him from spiritual unfaithfulness.*
   A. By discouraging Jacob's continuance in spiritual apostasy.
      1. He forgot his vows at Bethel.
      2. He failed to put God first as he had promised. There were places and times when there were no evidences of worship.
      3. He robbed God of the tithe that was His.
      4. His family even became associated with idolatry.
   B. By calling Jacob back to Bethel.
      1. For a time of rededication and renewal.
      2. To a new joy in service.
      3. To perfect that which God had begun (Philippians 1:6).

V. *Redeemed him from the fear of death.*
   A. In spite of the fact that death is one of man's basic fears.
      1. Man may seek to appear rough and tough, but death strips away this veneer.
      2. Death is not a popular subject, but it is a relevant one.
   B. In spite of Jacob's limited knowledge about the future life.

C. Teaching Jacob that death does not exclude one from fellowship with God.
   1. He saw God's work as continuing. "Behold, I die: But God . . . " (48:21).
   2. He saw death as a reunion with a godly father and grandfather (47:30).
   3. He knew that even in death he would be with God. Do you?

VI. *Redeemed him from the uncertainty of the future.*
(Men worry about the future. They wonder about the world situation and personal problems.)

A. Jacob learned that the future is in God's hand (48:21).
   1. God would be there in Egypt.
   2. God would return them to the land.
   3. God would preserve them for Himself.

B. Jacob was certain of his redemption that would continue in the future, and he proclaimed it.

51

Having Faith in the Future

Genesis 49:1-33

In 1938 Orson Wells produced a radio play in which he described an invasion of our world by invaders from Mars. So realistic was it that people believed it was true. Many thought the end of the world had come. Scores of people committed suicide and multitudes were deeply worried.

Today we live in a worried and troubled age. In our own country, civil disobedience has been given the stamp of acceptability and respectability. In Korea the cessation of hostilities in 1953 failed to solve the problems in Asia. MacArthur insisted that "there is no substitute for victory," but he was not heeded. In Vietnam, conflicts continue. Throughout Southeast Asia there is strife. In the Middle East, swords continue to rattle. As we look up and around we see that the signs of the latter times are everywhere. Our Lord may return at any moment. But as people think of the future, the end of the world, and the return of Christ, they are troubled. Christ intends that His promised return is to bring peace, not perplexity. We are admonished to "rejoice, for your redemption draweth nigh."

Jacob was looking into the future. Realizing that his remaining days were few, he spoke to his sons of the future and of their futures. His words contained the true ring of faith.

Having faith in the future:

I. *Requires a critical look at the past.*

A. To know the past provides a helpful guide concerning the future.

1. When Simon Peter spoke of the coming destruction of the world by fire, he wrote of its past destruction by the flood. (Noah and his day have much to tell us about future judgment).

2. When Jacob spoke of the future of his sons he referred to their past sins and activities which characterized their lives.

a. Reuben (49:3-4). He had an immoral past; he faced an unstable future.

(1) Reuben was Jacob's first-born.

(2) Yet he forfeited his blessing by his unholy conduct.

b. Simeon and Levi (49:5-7).

(1) They were guilty of gross inhumanity and cruelty against the Shechemites.

(2) They would lack a permanent settlement in the land.

c. Judah (49:8-12).

(1) Judah discovered the spiritual consequences of sin.

(2) He became the tribe of Messianic blessing (49:10).

d. Zebulun (49:13). Doubtless he was attracted to ships and trading.

(2) This helped determine his tribal location on the Mediteranean Sea.

e. Joseph (49:22-26).

(1) He had proven himself under the most adverse conditions.

(2) He would possess the blessings of the covenant.

B. To try to understand the future while ignoring the past is futile.

II. *Provides hope concerning the future* (49:10, 18).

A. Jacob looked hopefully ahead to Canaan, though he was living in Egypt.

B. Jacob looked hopefully ahead to eternity, though he was abiding in time.

C. Jacob looked hopefully ahead to the Messiah.

1. Who would come through Judah's line.
2. Who would reign over the whole house of Israel.
3. Who would unite all peoples under His universal rule.

D. Jacob's profession of faith was made in and to God (49:18).

1. It was not a salvation of works, but of grace.
2. It was not of man's doings, but of God's giving.

E. Jacob looked forward ultimately to the cross in faith.

1. There are not two ways of salvation, but only one.
2. We look back to the cross in the same way by a commitment of self to Christ.

III. *Results from a personal faith in the present* (49:29, 33).

A. Jacob's life had been used to instruct his sons concerning God.

1. With some of them he seemingly failed at the time, but a tribe of Israel came from each one. ("Train up a child in the way he should go. . ." Proverbs 22:6.)
2. With some of his sons he wonderfully succeeded.
3. Our life is also to be used as a witness to others.

B. Jacob's view of death was as a friend, for he was going to be with his father, and with God.

1. He overcame its fear. (John Wesley said, "Our people die well.")
2. Death is real, but it is a door through which we may walk into the arms of God, or from Him into hell.
3. Our destiny is determined by our decision today.

Illustration:

A dying father had three sons, one of whom was wayward. The father said to two of them, "So long, son, I'll see you in the morning." To the third son he said, "Good-bye." When the son realized the different farewell, he asked, "Why did you make such a difference?" The father replied, "Because you have failed to trust our Lord. Your brothers I expect to see again, but I fear that I shall not see you." As a result he, too, trusted Christ as his Lord.

52

Faith's Impressions on Life

Genesis 50

A missionary had gone into the Louisiana marsh and preached in a home where several families had gathered. One couple who had nine children made a profession of faith and surrendered their hearts to Christ. They asked their pastor if he would pick them up the next Sunday that they might attend church. When he arrived the following Sunday, the husband invited him in, explaining that they had something they needed to discuss with him. They said, "We are not married, and this is not right for Christians to live together unmarried. We want to be baptized, but would you marry us first?" That afternoon, with all nine children and other relatives in attendance, they celebrated a church wedding. That night they experienced believer's baptism! Faith makes a difference in life. It makes an impression.

Faith made impressions on Joseph's life in the following ways:

I. *Deepened the filial relationship* (50:1-6).
   A. Joseph and Judah enjoyed an exceptional closeness to Jacob.
      1. Even in light of the years Joseph was forcibly removed from his family.
      2. Even in light of his busy rounds of responsibilities.
   B. The relationship was deeper than mere blood ties.
      1. As seen in Joseph, the son of beloved Rachel.
         a. He developed a deep appreciation for the covenant's spiritual blessings.
         b. He desired these blessings for his children.
         c. He experienced a meaningful relationship with Jacob.
      2. As seen in Judah.
         a. In spite of his sinful past.
         b. In light of his spiritual development.
            (1) Benjamin was entrusted to his care, not to Reuben.
            (2) The messianic blessings were channeled through him.
   C. As children we all have responsibilities to our parents, but as Christians our responsibilities are made greater.
      1. We cannot ignore the Fifth Commandment (Exodus 20:12) with impunity.
      2. As one's parents grow older the responsibility becomes even greater.
         a. It may involve a visit, a call, or a letter.
         b. It must include an expressed interest. (A young man was excluded by his family after he was converted. Later, how-

ever, because of his concern for his parents, they became closer than ever to him. His mother requested that he preach his father's funeral that they might hear him preach for the first time.)

D. As parents we have a responsibility to deserve such honor.
   1. Many parents are run by their children.
   2. The modern home has been defined as "a place where everything is run by switches except the children."
   3. The modern child at age four has all the questions, and at age fourteen has all the answers.
   4. Parents are not to despair, but should begin early to nurture their children in Christian growth.

II. *Heightened family responsibilities* (50:7-9, 12-13).
   A. Joseph attended and participated in his father's burial.
      1. He could have "begged off."
      2. He had many weighty responsibilities.
   B. The others could have performed the burial without him.
   C. The Christian has a responsibility to manifest Christ to other family members by accepting responsibilities.

III. *Extended forgiveness for wrongs suffered* (50:15-18, 21).
   A. Joseph's pure motives were misconstrued and his intentions distorted.
      1. Joseph's brethren misunderstood him.
         a. At Potiphar's house or in prison we have no record that Joseph cried.
         b. But at this time Joseph wept.
      2. They were anxious regarding their own future.
   B. Joseph's forgiveness was genuine and real. (His heart provided no harbor for malice. Bitter enmity could find no refuge in his soul.)
   C. Families may expect misunderstandings and difficulties. (Brothers and sisters look at the same situation from varying viewpoints.)
      1. Forgiveness is the basis for happy family fellowship.
      2. In a certain family one of its members did not receive as expensive a Christmas gift as he had given. He just cut himself off from them even though he claimed to love Jesus.
      3. "To err is human; to forgive is divine."
      4. "And be ye kind one to another, tenderhearted, forgiving one another, even as God for Christ's sake hath forgiven you" (Ephesians 4:32).

IV. *Added purpose to life* (50:19-20, 24-25).
   A. Order and purpose may be seen throughout our world: in the solar system, in atoms, and in snowflakes.
   B. Some eyes are too blind to see purpose in life.
   C. Joseph, however, saw a divine purpose in his life. (It combined the bitter and the sweet.)

1. There is purpose in the present: to witness for God.
   a. Sharing one's faith. (Is a faith unable to be communicated worth anything?)
   b. Demonstrating one's maturity in his potential for reproduction.
2. There is purpose in the past: to learn and prepare for present tests.
   a. In the pit, in Potiphar's house, and in prison, Joseph learned lessons that were invaluable in his work as premier.
   b. In keeping with his father's example, Joseph rejoiced in the marvelous grace of God.
3. There is purpose in the future: waiting for God to work to His glory.
   a. His hope was in a full and meaningful future.
   b. His children were to share in it.
   c. His spirit would "be in that number" when God's people entered the Promised Land.

V. *Developed a fearlessness toward death* (50:25-26).
  A. Joseph did not view death as the end.
    1. He looked beyond the immediate moment.
    2. He viewed the prospect of eternity.
  B. Joseph rejoiced in God's promised intervention.
    1. For Joseph the question was not *if,* but *when* would God visit them.
    2. For us as we look to the Blessed Hope we continue to ask not *if,* but *when,* and rejoice in it.
       a. We have the assurance that "I may not be what I ought to be, and I am not what I'm going to be, but I know I'm not what I used to be."
       b. We have the promise that as God perfected the faith of His followers before us, so He will perfect us and all others who believe in Him (cf., Philippians 1:6).